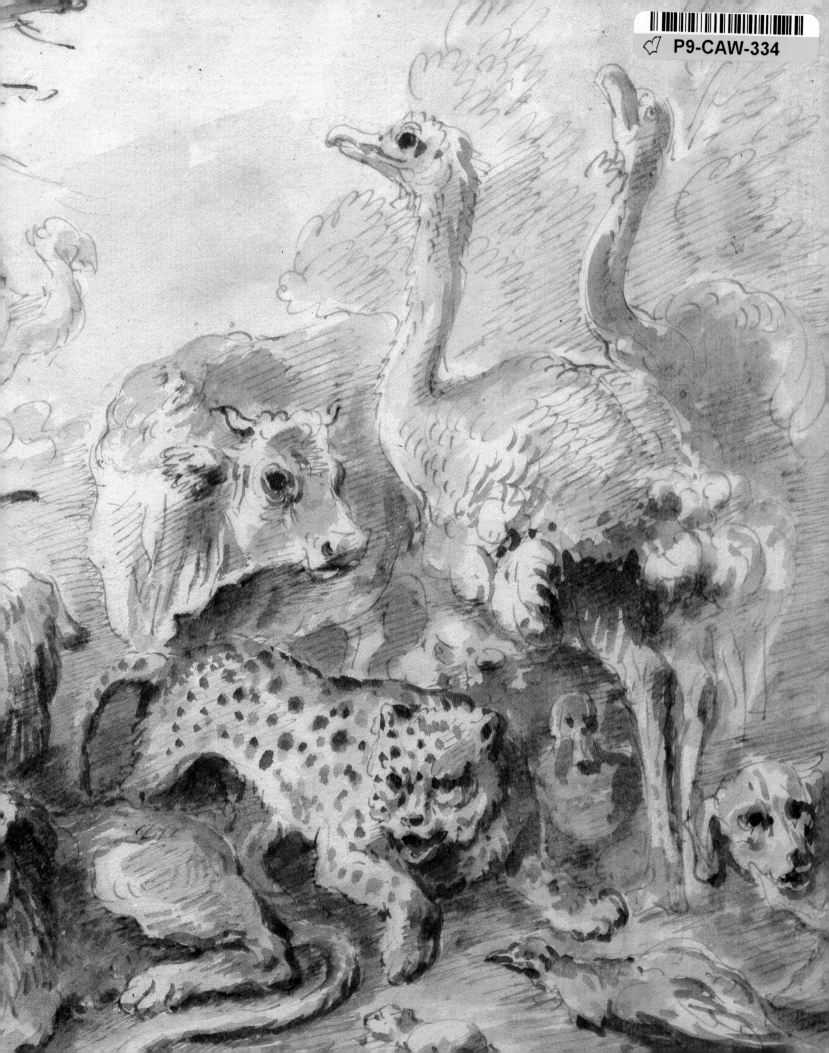

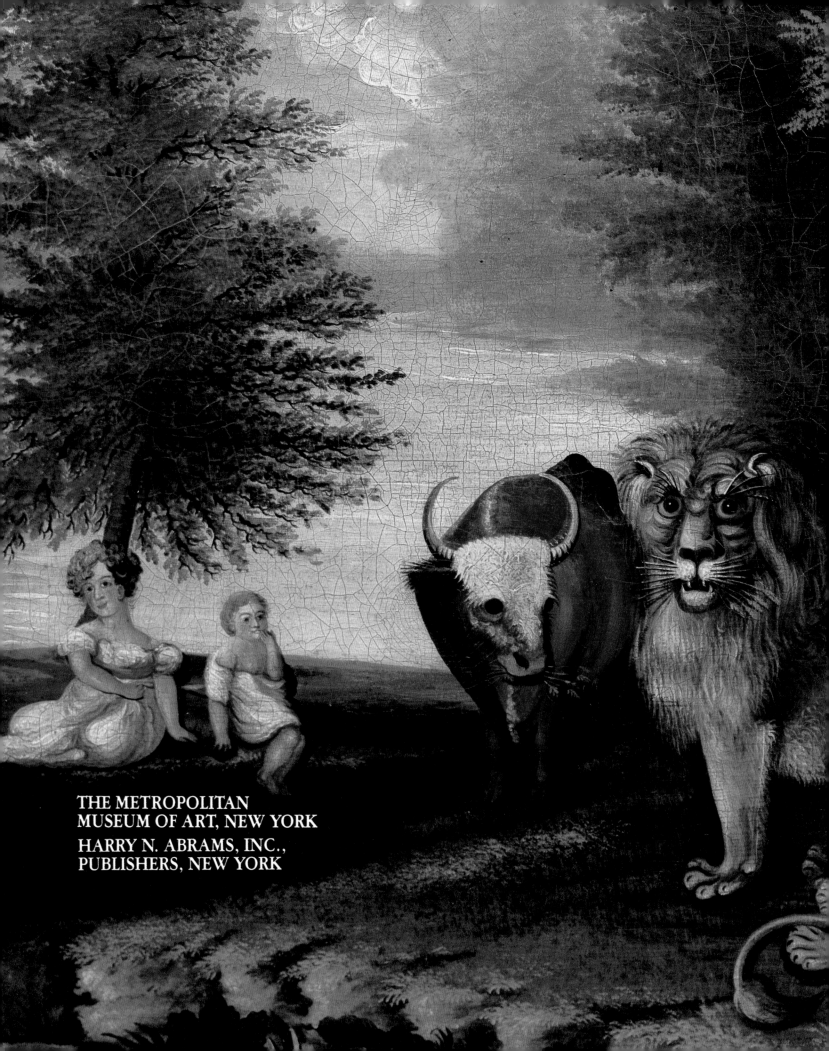

THE METROPOLITAN
MUSEUM OF ART, NEW YORK

HARRY N. ABRAMS, INC.,
PUBLISHERS, NEW YORK

METROPOLITAN ZOO

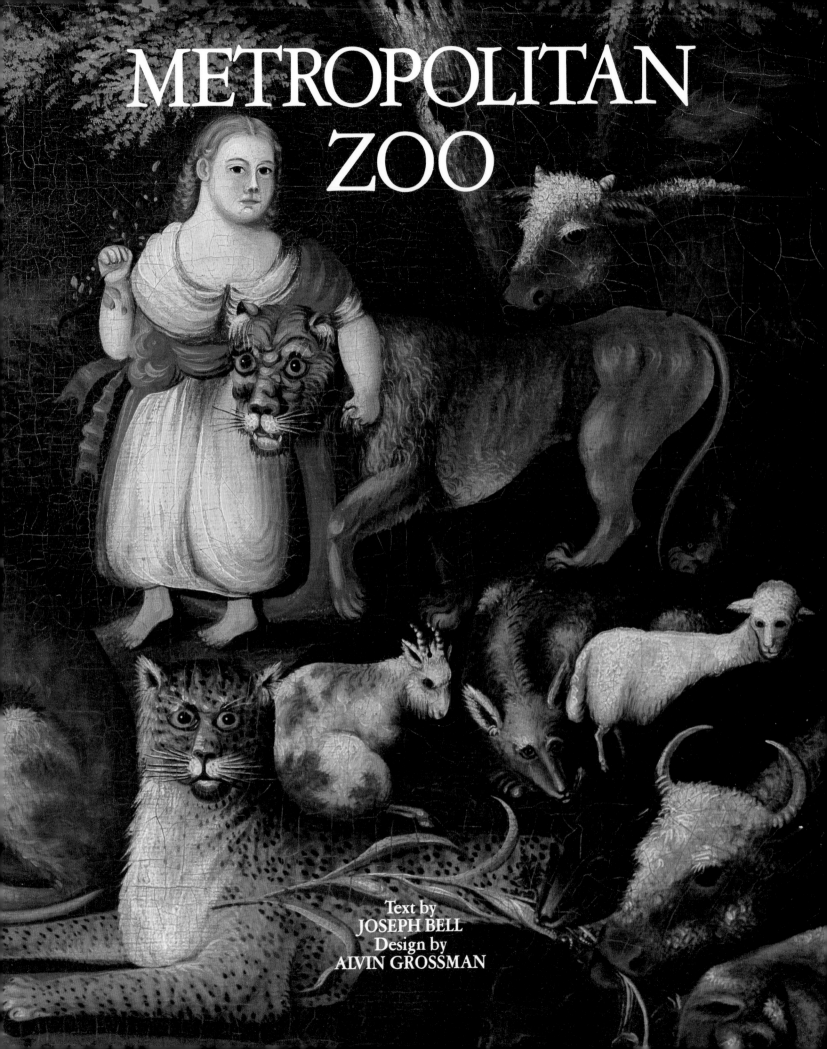

Text by
JOSEPH BELL
Design by
ALVIN GROSSMAN

Published by The Metropolitan Museum
of Art, New York
Bradford D. Kelleher, Publisher
John P. O'Neill, Editor in Chief
Barbara Burn, Project Supervisor
Alvin Grossman, Designer
Cynthia Clark, Editor

Library of Congress Cataloging in Publi-
cation Data

Bell, Joseph L., 1921–
Metropolitan zoo.

1. Animals in art. 2. Metropolitan Museum of Art (New York, N.Y.) I. Grossman, Alvin. II. Metropolitan Museum of
Art (New York, N.Y.) III. Title.
N7662.B45 1985   704.9′432   85-10633

ISBN 0-87099-430-1 (MMA)
ISBN 0-8109-1417-4 (HNA)

The photographs for this volume were
taken by the Photograph Studio of The
Metropolitan Museum of Art, with the exception of those on pages 5, 26, 33, 40–41,
44 right, which were taken by Malcolm
Varon, and those on pages 2–3, 21 top left,
24 bottom, 32 top left, 34 top, 37 right, 38
left, 42, 45, 47 bottom, 56 top, 57, 63, 64,
65 top, 65 bottom, 70, 71 top, 71 bottom,
73 left, 74 top, 81, 82, 83 bottom, 84–85,
87 bottom right, 88 bottom, 92 top, 94, 95
left, 95 right, 96, 97 bottom, 98, 100 left,
and the endpapers, which were taken by
Bob Hanson.

Composition by The Graphic Word Inc.,
New York

Printed and bound by Dai Nippon Printing
Co., Ltd., Tokyo, Japan

TITLE PAGE: **Peaceable Kingdom** is the
ageless hope of mankind, a world in
which all creatures live in harmony.
Edward Hicks (American, 1780–
1849), a Pennsylvania Quaker lay
preacher, painted it just as Isaiah had
prophesied in the Old Testament, a
place where "the wolf also shall dwell
with the lamb, and the leopard shall lie
down with the kid . . . and a little child
shall lead them." Hicks was a painter of
shop signs and carriage bodies by
trade, and he was gifted with both a
keen sense of design and a vivid imagination. One of the most highly regarded of American "primitive"
artists, he painted *The Peaceable Kingdom* more than sixty times and gave
some of these works to his friends as
gifts.

OPPOSITE: **The Unicorn at the Fountain.** In this detail from the second
tapestry of a Franco-Netherlandish
series depicting the Hunt of the Unicorn, woven around 1500, we see a
stag, a pair of pheasants, rabbits,
hounds, and a hyena against a rich
background of foliage and flowers.
Along with a group of hunters, they
are watching the unicorn dip its horn
into water in an act of purification.
The tapestries, which may have been
made in celebration of a wedding, are
rich in Christian and secular imagery,
and each animal undoubtedly has a
reason for its presence—the stag perhaps because it was a favorite quarry of
hunters as well as a common symbol of
man's finest traits, the pheasant pair
symbolizing love, the rabbits fertility,
the hounds fidelity, and the hyena, by
contrast, symbolizing the Devil and
man's wickedness.

OVERLEAF: **Blind Men and the Elephant.** The search for truth is often
clouded by one's interpretation of
facts; thus the individual conclusions
of the blind men in this charming Japanese netsuke will all differ depending
on the part of the animal each has ex-
plored. Truth combined with good
judgment is wisdom, and, by sharing
knowledge, even blind men can de-
scribe an elephant accurately. This
ancient but still sound philosophy is
expressed clearly and humorously
in this tiny ivory carving by the nineteenth-century master carver Kuku
Josō. Elephants have fascinated the
Japanese for hundreds of years and often appeared in early Buddhist paintings and sculptures. A netsuke is used
to secure the cord of a tobacco pouch
or medicine receptacle to the belt.

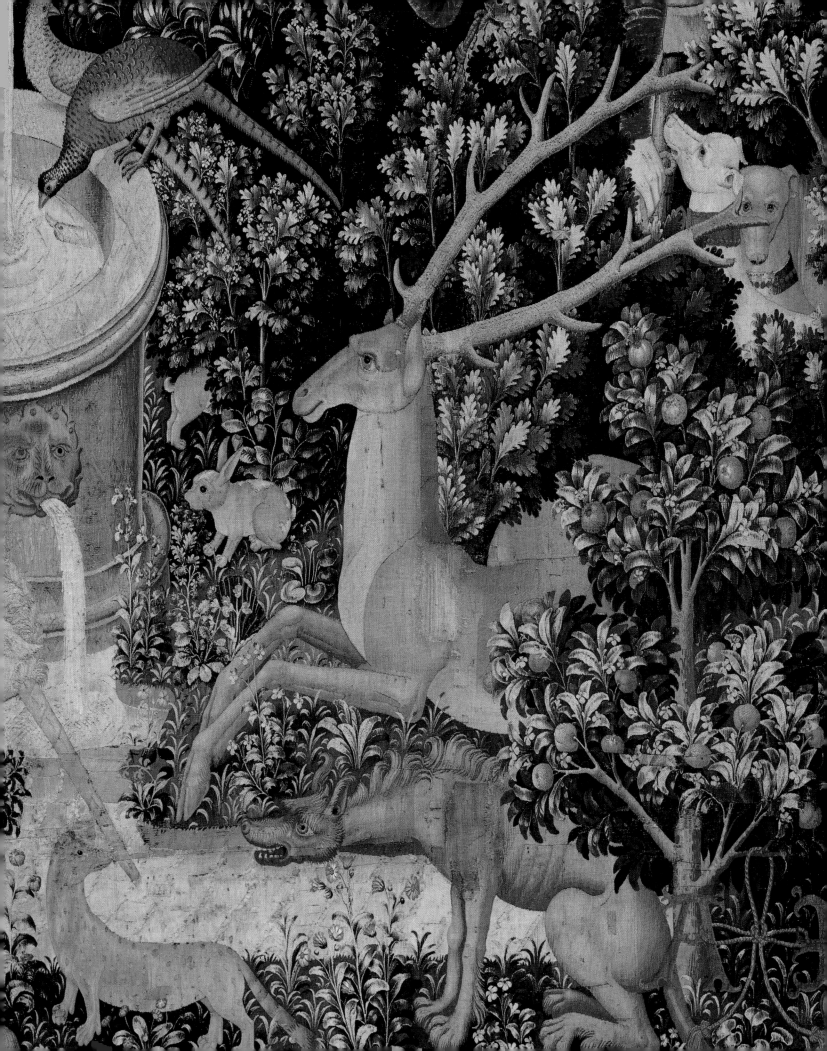

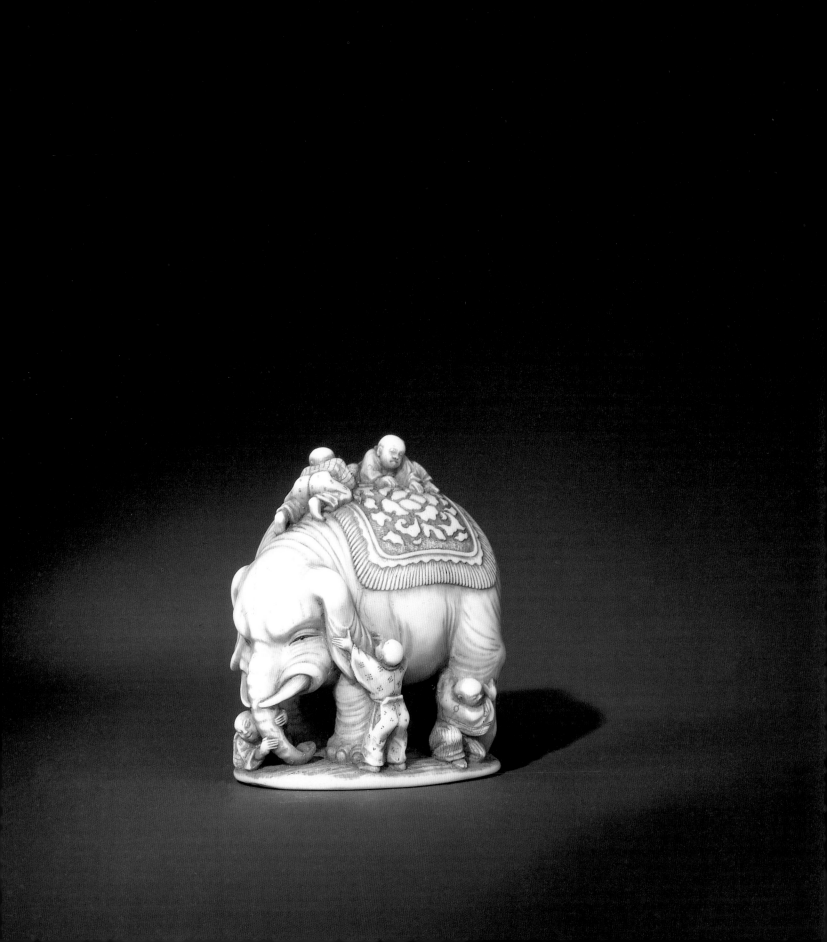

Introduction

Within the pages of this book exists a fascinating zoological garden. Not only does it host a fine collection of wild creatures from every land—most zoos do that—but it also includes animals that look just as they once did to people of many historical periods and cultures. The animals are represented here in paintings, drawings, sculpture, and innumerable other media: lions of glazed brick from ancient Babylon, frogs of gold from Precolumbian America, kangaroos on bark from northern Australia, and bats delicately embroidered on Chinese ceremonial robes.

The history of animals in art can be traced to the Paleolithic era, when Stone Age hunters engraved and painted primitive but recognizable outlines of antelope and bison, among other prey species, on the walls of caves. What motivated these people to make the pictures is unknown, but they certainly depended on animals for food and clothing, found them difficult to pursue and kill, and undoubtedly admired them for their strength and speed. It seems reasonable to assume that this esteem may have been the basis for the veneration of animals by most primitive cultures, even those of recent times, as in Africa, Australia, and the Americas. The ancient Egyptians represented many of their gods in animal forms, yet there and in many other civilizations objects and paintings depicting animals seem to have no religious or symbolic significance but result simply from man's natural inclination to select subjects from the world around him. Although the first figurative images were of animals, these forms later became secondary or subordinate to depictions of humans, although in several cultures specialized types of art featuring animals developed, such as the bird-and-flower paintings of China or the animal portraits of Western Europe. As decorative elements, animals were often subjected to severe stylization, making positive identification difficult or impossible, but from the famous cave paintings of Lascaux to the exquisite wood engravings of Utamaro, naturalistic renderings have often been nearly scientifically accurate.

The history of animals in captivity is equally difficult to trace. Man certainly took up the husbandry of wild animals soon after he ceased to be one himself. Domestic cattle, swine, horses, and barnyard fowl were all developed from wild stock long before any written record was made. Nonfood species, such as dogs and cats, were also domesticated thousands of years ago, as companions, guards, hunting or herding partners, or as objects of beauty and curiosity. It was undoubtedly this last category that brought about the early menageries, in which wild animals were kept to amuse and entertain the curious but were neither tamed nor bred for any domestic purpose. The modern zoological park is a far cry from these early menageries of the ruling or aristocratic classes, both in its accommodations for animals and in the philosophy that sustains it. Gone are the old iron bars, which have been replaced by naturalistic habitat settings where hidden moats separate the visitor from the animals. Curiosity and the desire to be entertained may still bring people into a zoo, but the primary function of zoo curators, as of their counterparts in art museums, is to make the visit a learning experience, whether for the specialist or for the general public. Through zoos people may learn to understand nature and the importance of conserving wild things. As natural habitats in the wild are destroyed, zoo curators breed endangered species in captivity to continue their existence on earth, so that future civilizations will not have to rely on books like this one to see what animals of the past actually looked like.

Because the Museum's holdings are so vast, we decided to omit all of the domestic species here and to concentrate instead on wild animals, which have intrigued artists of so many periods and cultures. It is interesting to note, incidentally, that a number of the artists represented here have relied on captive collections or zoos for the opportunity to study their subjects up close. Dürer's famous rhinoceros was based on a sketch made to record the arrival in Europe of one of the first Indian rhinos seen on the continent. Antoine-Louis Barye and Jean-Léon Gérôme regularly visited the Jardin des Plantes in Paris, and Henri Rousseau drew many of his fantastic scenes from photographs and drawings made in zoos. George Stubbs frequented a local menagerie keeper and visited English country gentlemen who kept wild animals on their estates. During the nearly four decades that I spent at the New York Zoological Park, the Zoo frequently welcomed artists—among them Alexander Calder and Anna Hyatt Huntington—as they made their sketches.

As curator of ornithology at the Zoo, I found myself acting as a guide for groups of people of all ages, personally taking them through the collection. This is the first time, however, when my knowledge of the animals has had to be supplemented quite so extensively by curators from another institution. My gratitude to the curators and their staffs at The Metropolitan Museum of Art is immeasurable, and I am also grateful to the following for their assistance: John P. O'Neill for supporting the project enthusiastically, Barbara Burn for suggesting that I be the guide, Al Grossman for creating a wonderfully lively design appropriate to the subject, and Stephen Sechrist for his patience in seeing to all of the details.

Joseph Bell

Creation of the Animals. The fifth and sixth days of creation, according to the book of Genesis, were devoted to the animals. First, God caused "the waters to bring forth abundantly the moving creatures that hath life, and fowl that may fly above the earth in the open firmament of heaven." On the following day, God created the beasts of the earth, which is the scene depicted in this engraving by an unidentified Italian artist of the sixteenth century after a design by Raphael. The theory of evolution postulates that sea creatures were most likely the first living organisms on the planet—as the Bible implies—followed by amphibians, reptiles, birds, and, finally, mammals. But in this print, executed some three hundred years before Charles Darwin wrote his *Origin of Species,* evolution is nowhere evident. Not only is there a purely imaginary unicorn in the background, along with deer, camels, and an elephant, but there are also domesticated animals aplenty—cow, horse, dog, and rooster—each of them bred by man from wild species. Darwin himself might have been entertained by the notion of animals emerging fully formed from ooze and clouds, as they do here, but his favorite image would undoubtedly have been that of the monkey in the right foreground—a dead ringer for a human being!

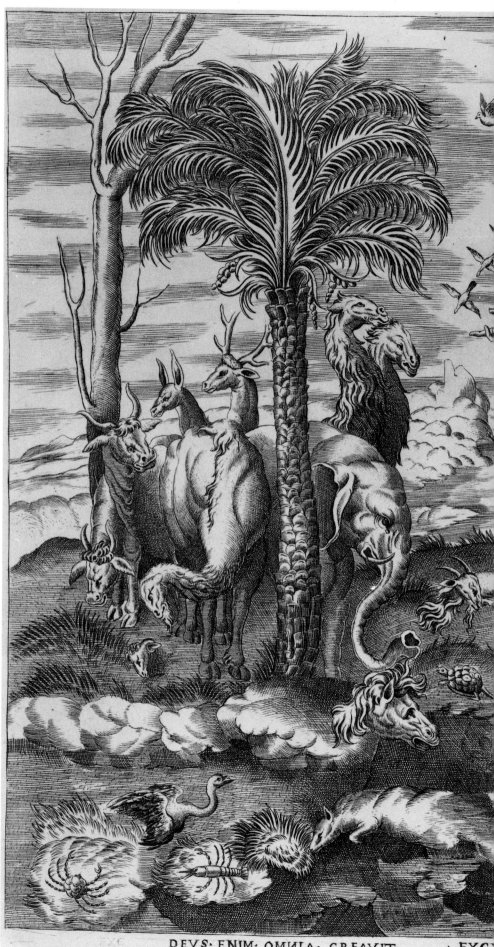

DEVS·ENIM·OMNIA·CREAVIT. · EXC

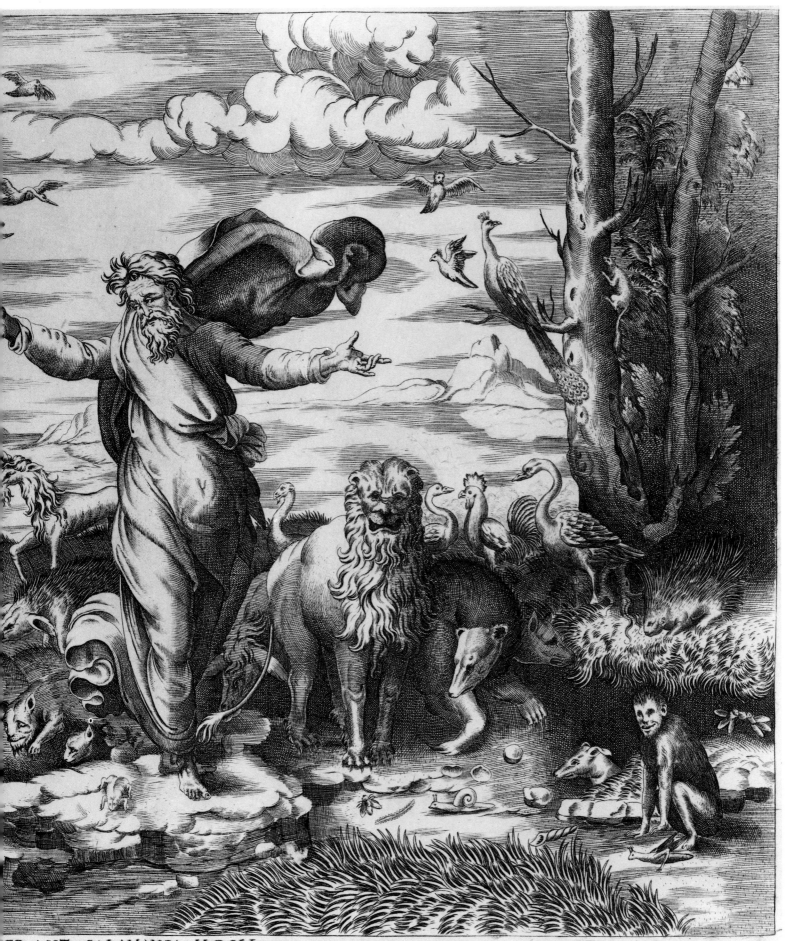

EB·ANT· SALAMANCA· M·D·X·L·

Noah's Ark. To save his family and all species of animals from destruction during the great flood, the book of Genesis tells us, six-hundred-year-old Noah constructed a gigantic boat to God's specifications in seven days. In this Currier and Ives lithograph, Noah and his sons can be seen escorting the animals aboard, two by two. Although Noah was commanded by God to bring every sort of animal into the ark, including ''every creeping thing,'' this print shows no reptile or amphibian of any kind, perhaps a reflection of the long-standing aversion of the general public to these animals. Nathaniel Currier began publishing prints in New York in 1840 and was joined by James Merritt Ives in 1852; the firm became Currier and Ives in 1857. For more than fifty years they produced several prints each week, most of them portraying scenes of American life during the nineteenth century but occasionally including popular biblical themes such as this one.

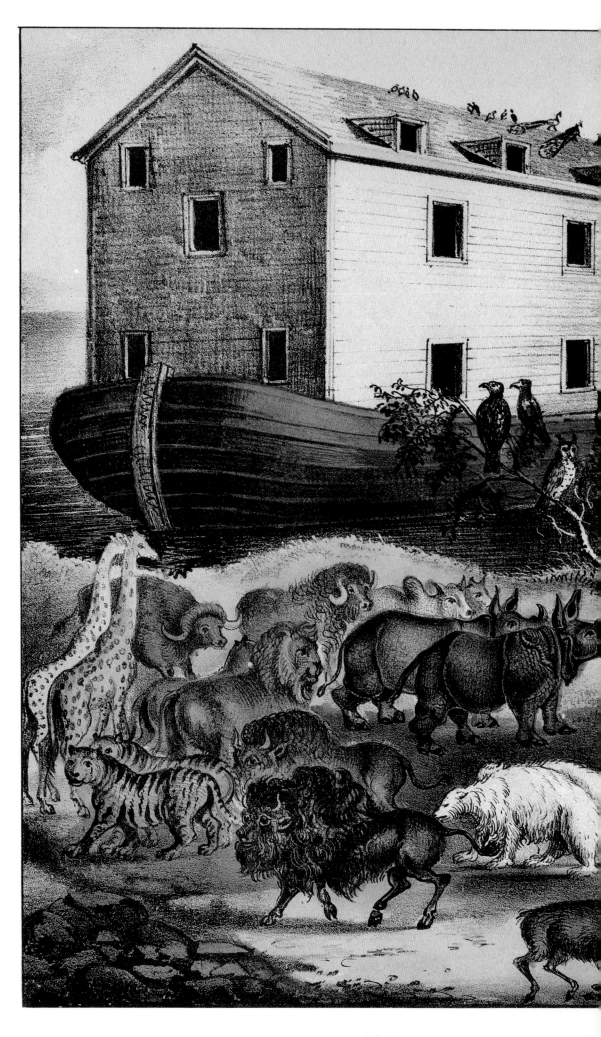

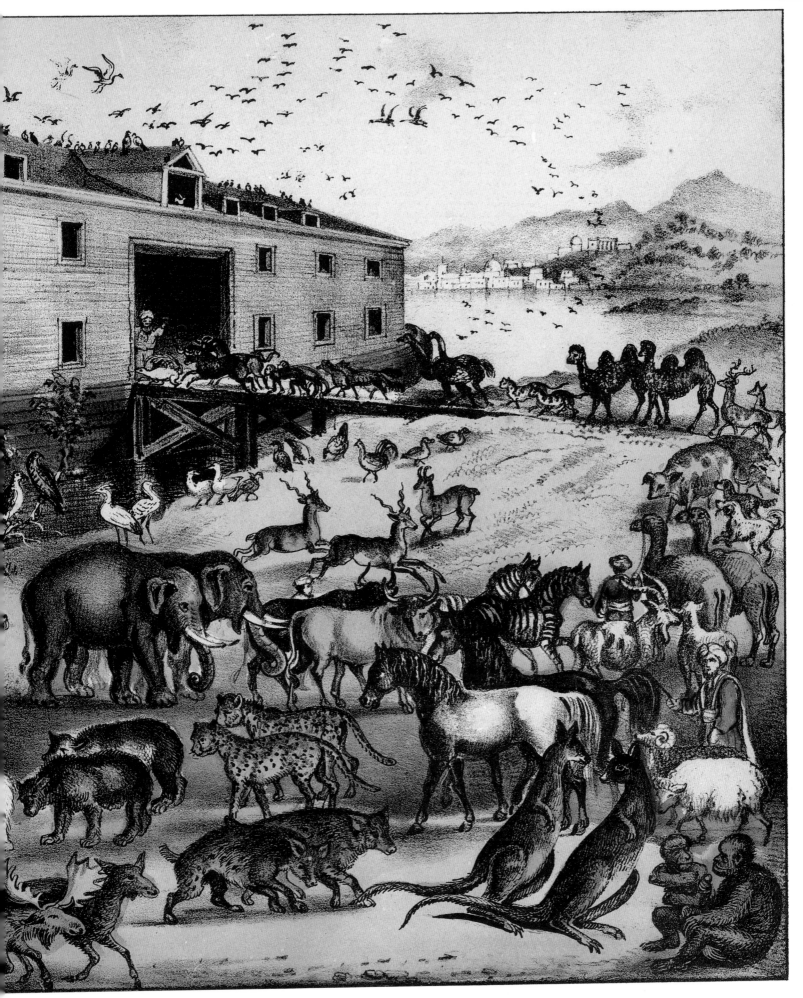

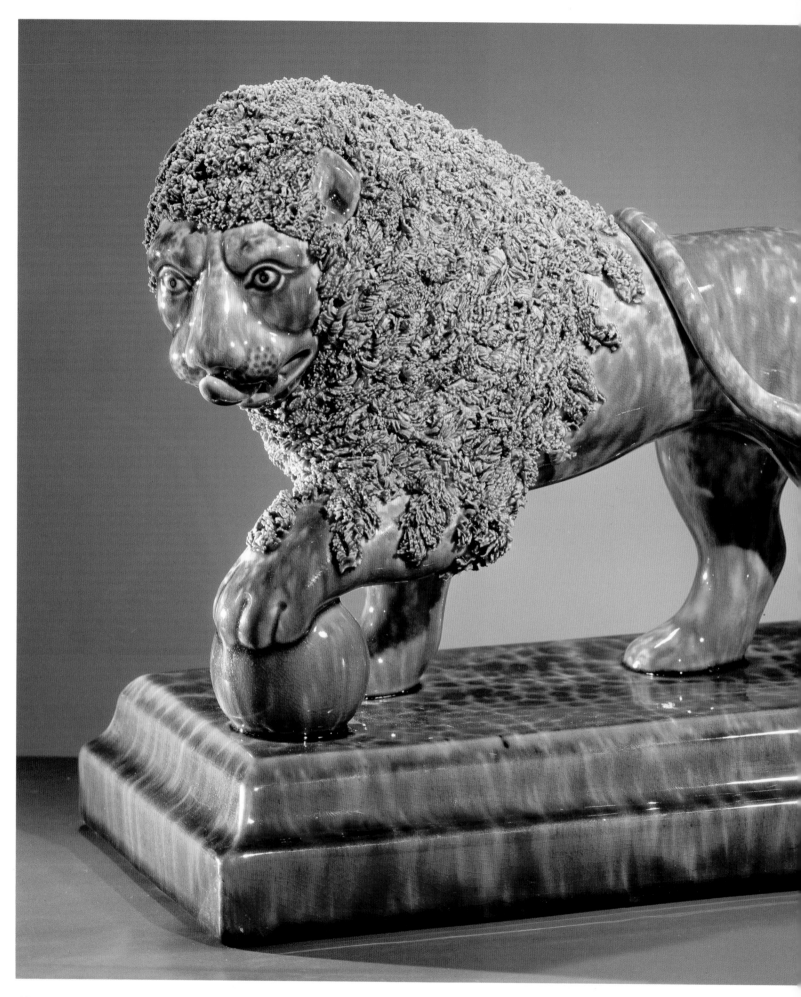

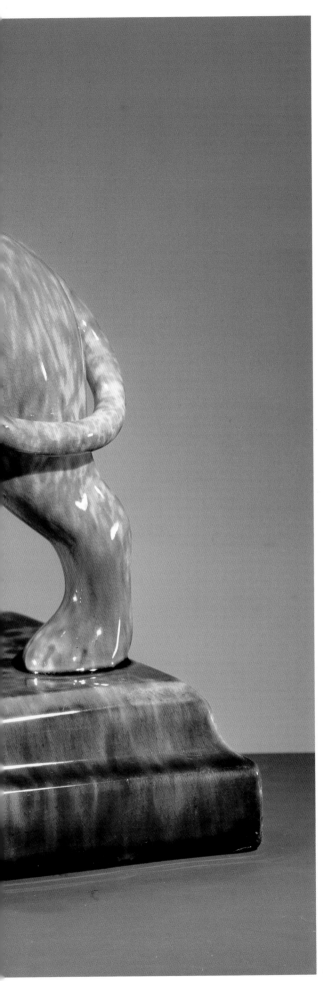

Figure of a Lion. Although this powerful, stylized animal study is reminiscent of lion statues produced during ancient and medieval times in Europe, Asia, and Africa, it is actually a nineteenth-century earthenware piece made by the United States Pottery Company in Bennington, Vermont. It was cast from a model prepared by Daniel Greatbach, who worked at Bennington from 1852 to 1858, and was finished with a flint enamel glaze, which gives it a wonderfully animated surface. The figure also resembles pottery lions produced in Staffordshire, England, and, while it is not known to be a direct copy, it features the same type of monumental base and "coleslaw" mane as the Staffordshire works. Popular not only as decorative and symbolic images, lions have also been favorites in menageries and zoos since the early ages. They reproduce readily in captivity, but inbreeding often results in physical deformities, such as the pug-nosed face on this Bennington lion.

Lion. The lion in the wood engraving below by Thomas Bewick (British, 1753–1828) is small in size but as grand in spirit as his counterparts in nature. Combining a keen interest in natural history with his skill as an artist, Bewick brought a lifelike quality to his animal illustrations. Some of his best works appear in *The General History of Quadrupeds* and *The History of British Birds.* By using a copperplate engraving tool on the end grain of a wood block, rather than the usual method of cutting into its longer and smoother side, Bewick perfected the delicate art of engraving on wood.

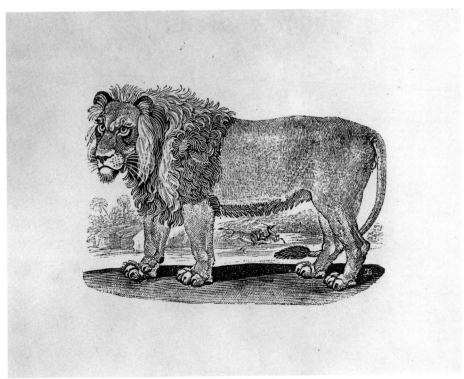

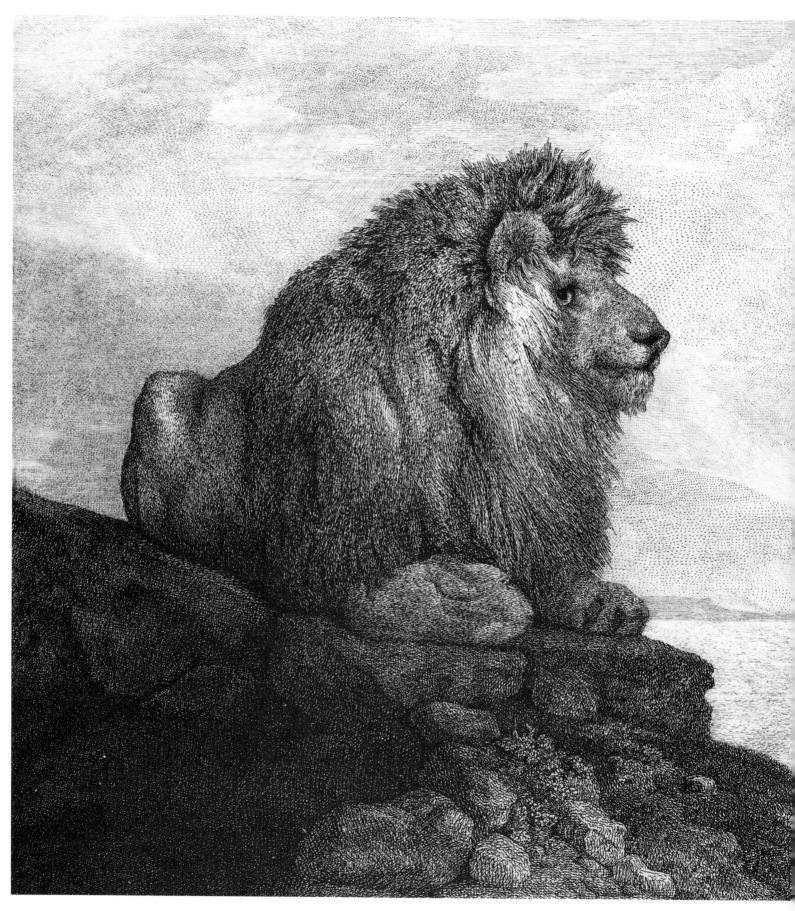

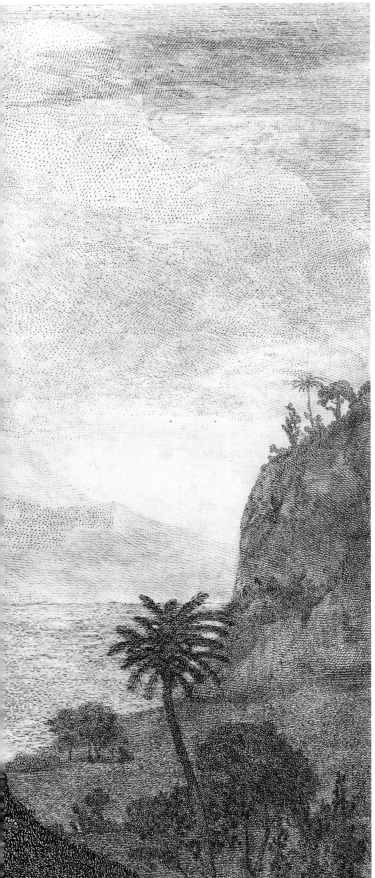

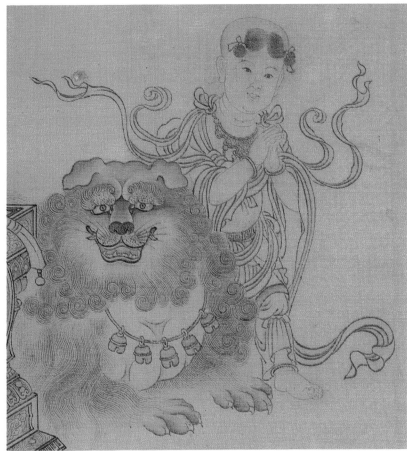

Vimalakirti Sutra. The fierce-looking lion and its young companion in this detail of a Chinese handscroll are attendants to Manjusri, the Bodhisattva of Wisdom, who is engaged in theological debate with a Confucian layman named Vimalakirti. The lion is considered sacred to the Buddhists, not only as a defender of the law, as it is here, but as a protector of sacred buildings. This scroll was painted in ink on silk by Wang Chen-p'eng (ca. 1280–1329), the leading exponent of ''plain drawing'' in both figural and architectural painting of the Yüan dynasty.

A Lion Resting on a Rock. This classic study of the king of beasts was made by the British artist George Stubbs (1724–1806). Best known for his paintings of horses, Stubbs had a lifelong interest in exotic species as well, including monkeys, rhinoceroses, zebras, and the great cats. The lion in this print was probably based on drawings Stubbs made of a live animal kept at the country estate of an English aristocrat. The print was published in 1788 as one of a group of twelve animal prints, another of which showed a lion attacking and devouring a frightened horse, a recurrent theme in Stubbs's work.

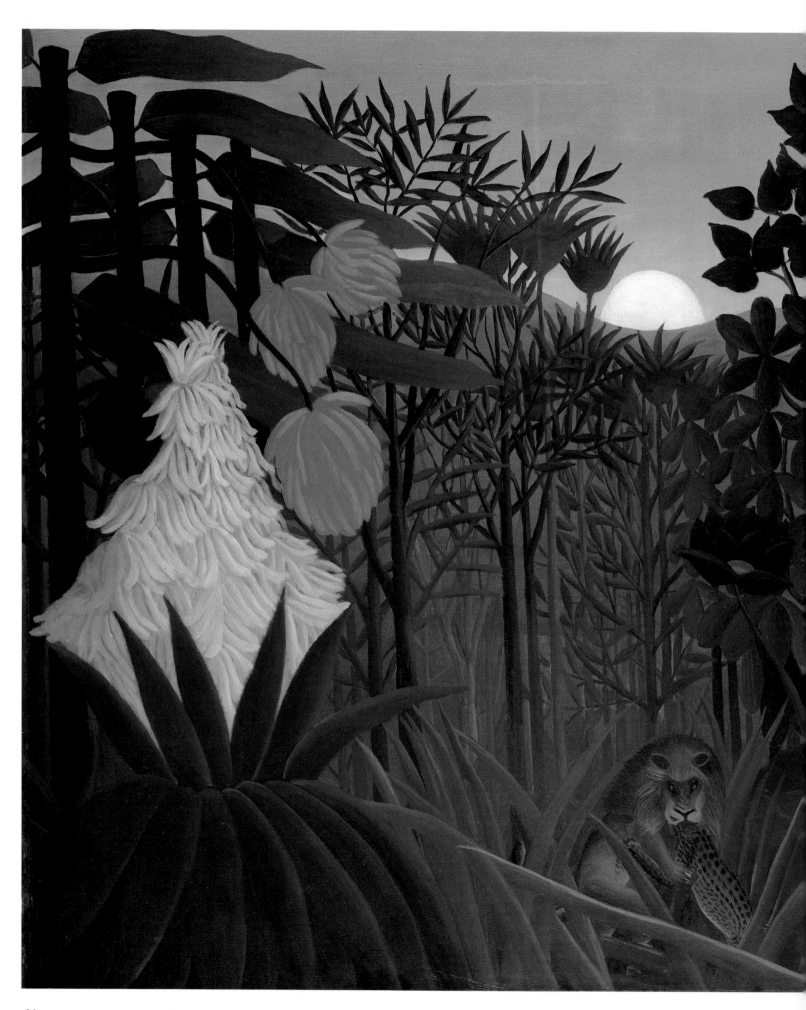

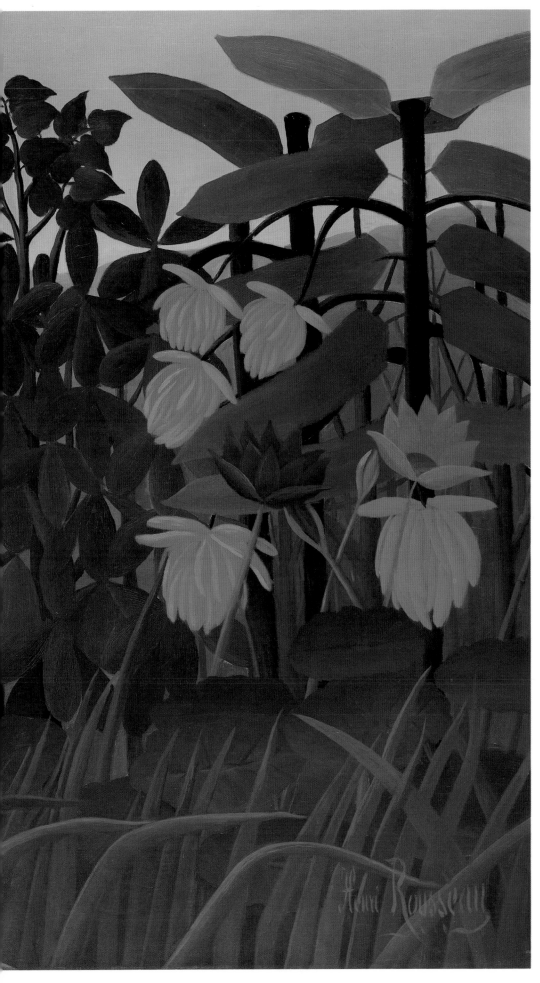

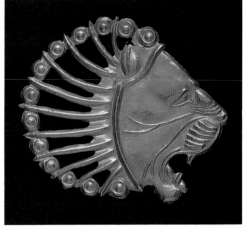

Lion-Head Appliqué. This delicate gold ornament from the Achaemenid period (550–332 B.C.) of ancient Iran is fitted on the back with five rings by which it could be attached to a cloth garment or a tent hanging. Lions were once found throughout much of the Near East but are now confined to Africa below the Sahara, with the exception of a small relict population in the Gir Forest of northwestern India.

The Repast of the Lion. In the heart of the jungle a male lion feasts on his prey; he is surrounded by lush tropical vegetation and backlit by a rising full moon that adds an eerie, dreamlike quality to the scene. This painting, a product of the vivid imagination of the self-taught artist Henri Rousseau (French, 1844–1910), is one of a series of jungle pictures that he began to create in 1891. A tour of army duty in Mexico provided Le Douanier Rousseau with ideas for his settings, which he enhanced with tropical plants based on specimens he saw in the Paris botanical garden and with animals drawn from zoo photographs in a book published by a local art gallery, as well as from the works of Delacroix and other artists whom he admired. Rousseau painted boldly, using strong colors and distinct forms but showing little concern for reality. The foliage, for example, and the brightly colored flowers are huge in comparison with the animals. As fanciful as the setting itself is the fact that Rousseau has chosen to depict an African lion, a native of open grasslands, deep in the jungle devouring a jaguar, which is a hunter of equal ferocity and prowess and is found only in the Americas.

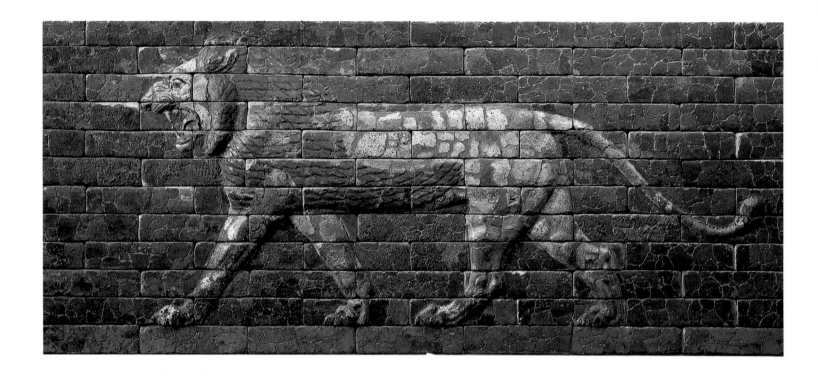

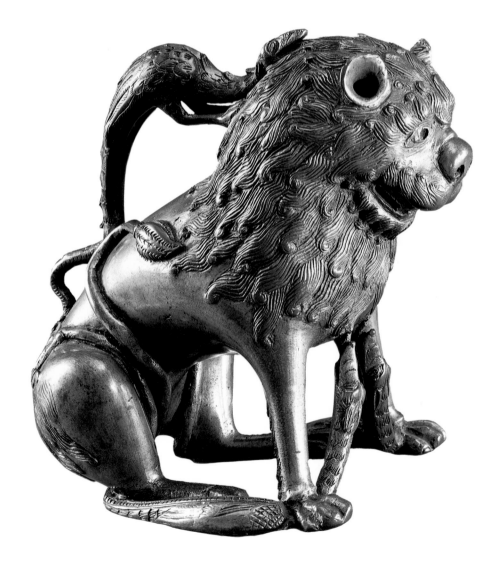

Panel with Striding Lion. During the reign of Nebuchadnezzar II (605–562 B.C.), the city of Babylon flourished. The majestic striding lion in the relief above is one of many that originally decorated the walls flanking the long processional road built by this great king. Stone was rare in southern Mesopotamia, so molded bricks, glazed in bright colors, were used to embellish the gates and buildings of cities. The lion was the symbol of Ishtar, the Mesopotamian goddess of love and war.

Lion Aquamanile. The thirteenth-century bronze water container at left is from northern Germany. Crafted in exaggerated animal forms, these jugs were used both in the home and in church during the celebration of the Mass. The lion would have been a most appropriate Christian image, for in medieval times he often appeared as the symbol of Christ and as an attribute of the apostle Saint Mark.

Parade Helmet. The ornate example of parade armor shown on the opposite page is Italian and dates to the mid-fifteenth century. Beneath its brilliant gilt-bronze surface, enhanced with inlaid semiprecious stones for the eyes and silvered teeth, is a serviceable polished-steel battle helmet. The gaping jaws of the lion, painted red inside, allowed the wearer to look out, presumably at the terrified face of his opponent, who would not have missed the fact that the form of the helmet resembled the skin of the Nemean lion that mighty Hercules wore as a headdress.

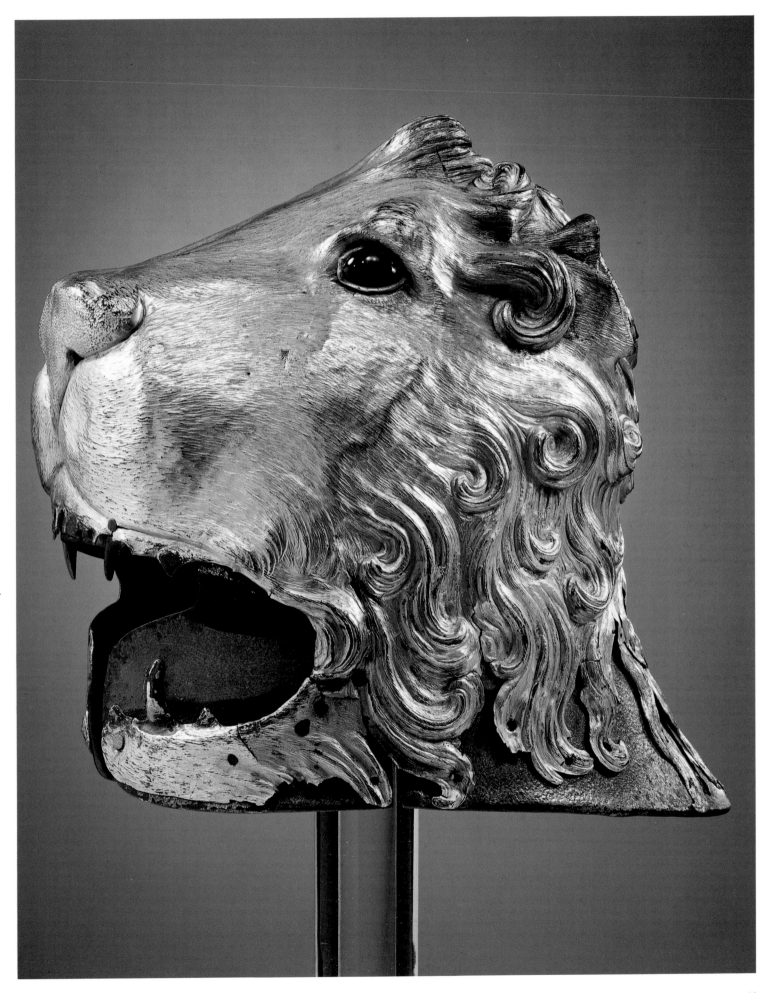

19

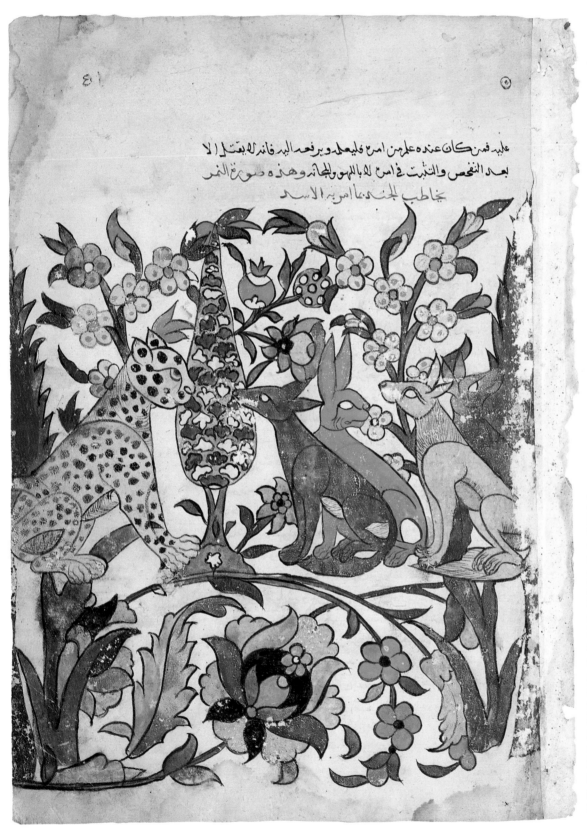

علیه فمن کان عنده علم من امره فلیعلم ویرفعه الید فانه لایقتل الا
بعد التفحص والتثبت فی اسم لا بالهوی والجهالة وهذه صورة النمر
یخاطب الجند ما اسریه الاسد

Kalila wa Dimna. "The Leopard Relating to His Fellow Judges What the Lion Has Ordered" is the title of the illustration shown at left, a leaf from a book of moralizing fables that probably dates to the mid-sixteenth century. Originally written in India, the stories were subsequently translated into Persian and Arabic and became popular throughout the Islamic world. This version is drawn with colors on paper and is written in Arabic.

Jaguar. Solemn and silent yet poised to spring, the largest of all the spotted cats peers with a baleful eye at something beyond our view in this pastel drawing on paper by British artist John Macallan Swan (1847–1910). After his early training at London's Royal Academy of Art, Swan continued to study animal anatomy in Paris under such masters as the painter Jean-Léon Gérôme and the sculptor Emmanuel Frémiet. Both leopards and jaguars have spots, but the latter, a native of South and Central America, is larger, and some of its rosette markings bear a characteristically dark central spot.

20

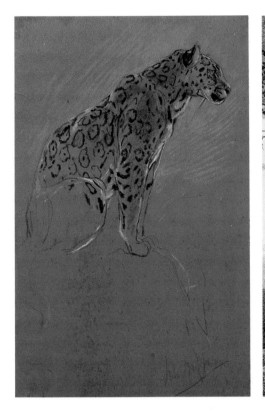

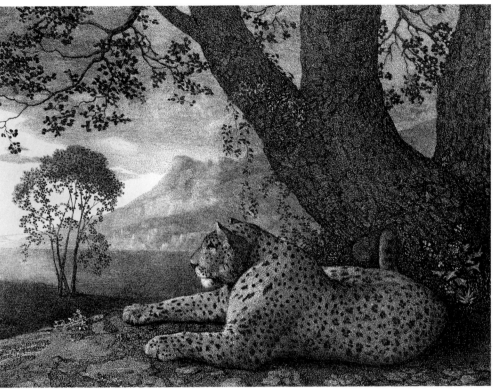

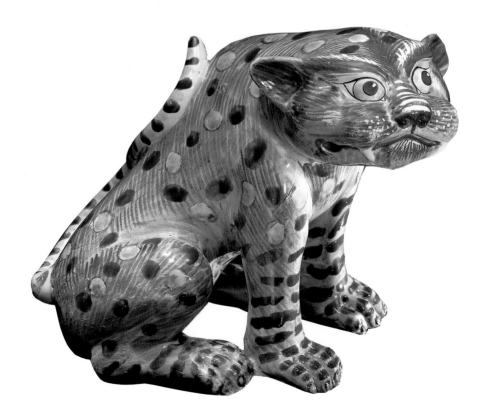

Recumbent Leopard by a Tree. Contented and well fed best describes the leopard in this print by George Stubbs. Using a mixed-method technique, the artist combined etching, engraving, and mezzotint to achieve a special tonal quality in the series of animal prints he published in 1788, of which this is one. Although he was well aware of the scientific differences between the various wild-cat species, Stubbs often referred to them all as ''tygers,'' a common practice in eighteenth-century England.

Chantilly Leopard. Looking more like the tabby cat that ate the canary than the bold, resourceful hunter of Asia and Africa, this soft-paste figure of a leopard was produced at the Chantilly factory near Paris about 1735. It is an adaptation of a rare porcelain tiger modeled in Japan at the end of the seventeenth century.

The Tyger. "Tyger, tyger burning bright / In the forests of the night." Using stealth and the cover of darkness to fullest advantage when stalking its quarry, the tiger is a predator with few peers. The English poet and painter William Blake (1757–1827) captured the essence of the great nocturnal hunter for all time on the page, below left, from his *Songs of Experience,* written in 1794 when Britain and France were at war.

Tiger. The colored engraving, below right, by Edward Julius Detmold (British, 1883–1957) also pictures the mighty cat at night, but here just the head is shown, profiled against a full moon. An engraver, watercolorist, and illustrator with a strong interest in exotic animals, Detmold was heavily influenced by Japanese art. The beautifully detailed feather below the tiger's head is from the orna-

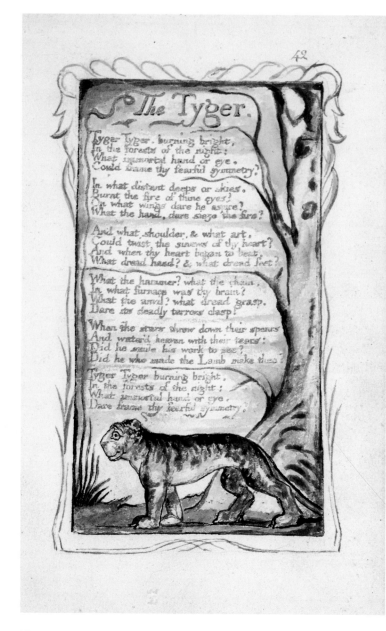

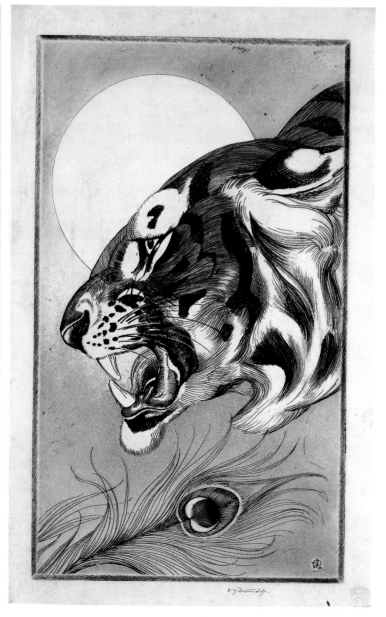

mental train of a peacock and appears to have been added for purely decorative reasons.

Tiger and Cubs. Alert but serene, a tigress watches over her sleepy cubs in this oil painting by the French painter Jean-Léon Gérôme (1824–1904). The artist's early experience studying live animals in the menagerie of the Jardin des Plantes in Paris no doubt accounts for the naturalistic treatment he gave them in paint. It is curious, however, that he has shown the cubs here as gray, when in fact they resemble adult tigers in coloration from birth. In the wild, tigers are solitary creatures, rarely coming together except to breed. The female raises her brood alone; one to four cubs is the normal litter. They may remain with her for about two years, when they are almost full grown and capable of hunting on their own.

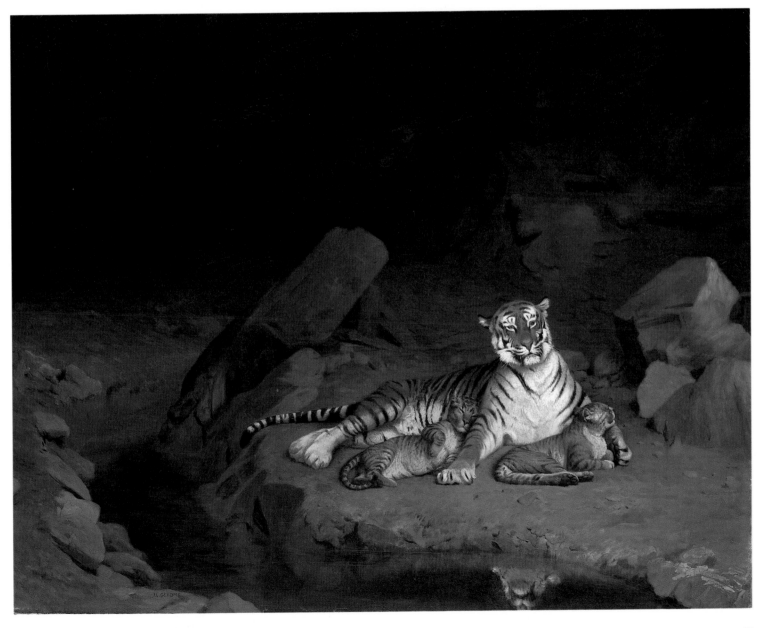

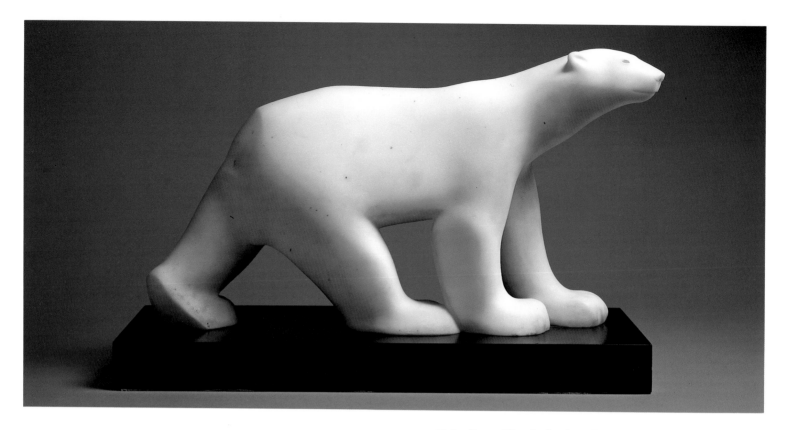

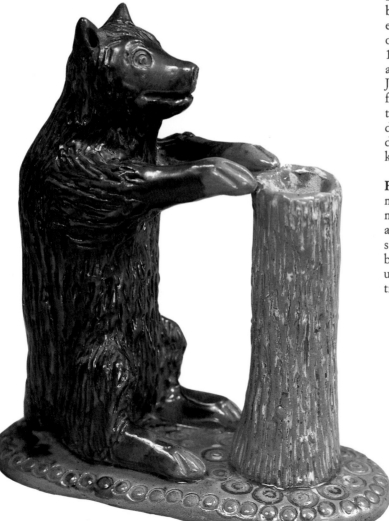

Polar Bear. The thick white fur and massive size of the polar bear make it a strikingly effective hunter on arctic ice and an extremely popular animal in zoological gardens. The sculptor of this handsome marble bear, François Pompon (French, 1855–1933), was a stone carver in Auguste Rodin's studio and a well-known animal artist who spent many a morning at the Jardin des Plantes in Paris sketching the animals in preparation for his sculpture. Deceptively simple in appearance, much like the polar bear itself, this piece was a great success at the Salon d'Automne of 1922; the subtle modeling of the stone clearly defines the animal's grace and strength and reflects the artist's knowledge of his subject.

Figure of a Bear and a Tree Stump. The unknown artist who made this piece of nineteenth-century Pennsylvania redware modeled his bear in much greater detail than Pompon. It probably represents an American black bear sitting at a hollow stump waiting for his chance to get some honey away from the bees within. This pose, a favorite with the general public, is unfortunately also typical of the begging posture assumed by trained bears in roadside zoos and carnivals.

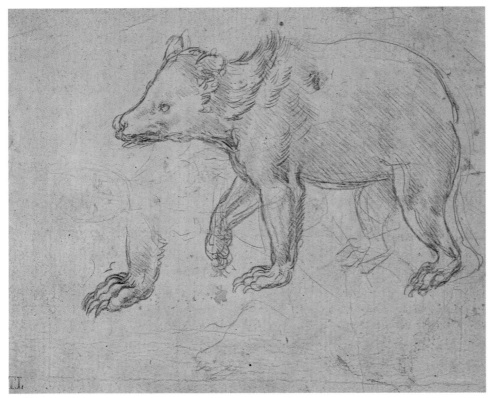

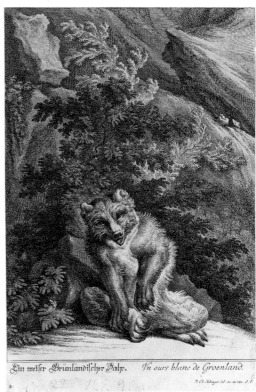

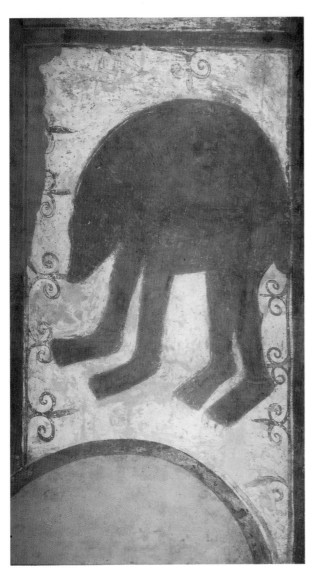

Study of a Bear Walking. Leonardo da Vinci (Italian, 1452–1519) rarely depicted animals other than horses, so this beautifully detailed study executed in silverpoint on light buff paper is of particular interest. Included is a separate study of the animal's right front foot that reveals the artist's fascination with anatomy. The faint image of a nude woman in the background indicates an earlier sketch on the same paper.

Bear. Most fanciful of all the bears on these pages is the one in the print shown above right by the German painter and engraver Johann Elias Ridinger (1698–1767). Sly looking, with a foxlike face and shifty eyes, this bear could easily be the villain in an old fairy tale. A woodman and hunter in his youth, Ridinger learned about animals through personal experience, and he later applied this knowledge to his interpretations of wildlife.

Bear Fresco. Whether they inhabit frozen wastes, rugged mountain slopes, or tropical forests, there is no mistaking a bear for any other animal. Even the simplified form in the Spanish fresco (left) retains the animal's basic characteristics: a heavy body, short ears and tail, and plantigrade feet with long nails. Originally painted in the church of San Bandelio in Berlanga, Spain, in the twelfth century, this fresco was later transferred to canvas and framed.

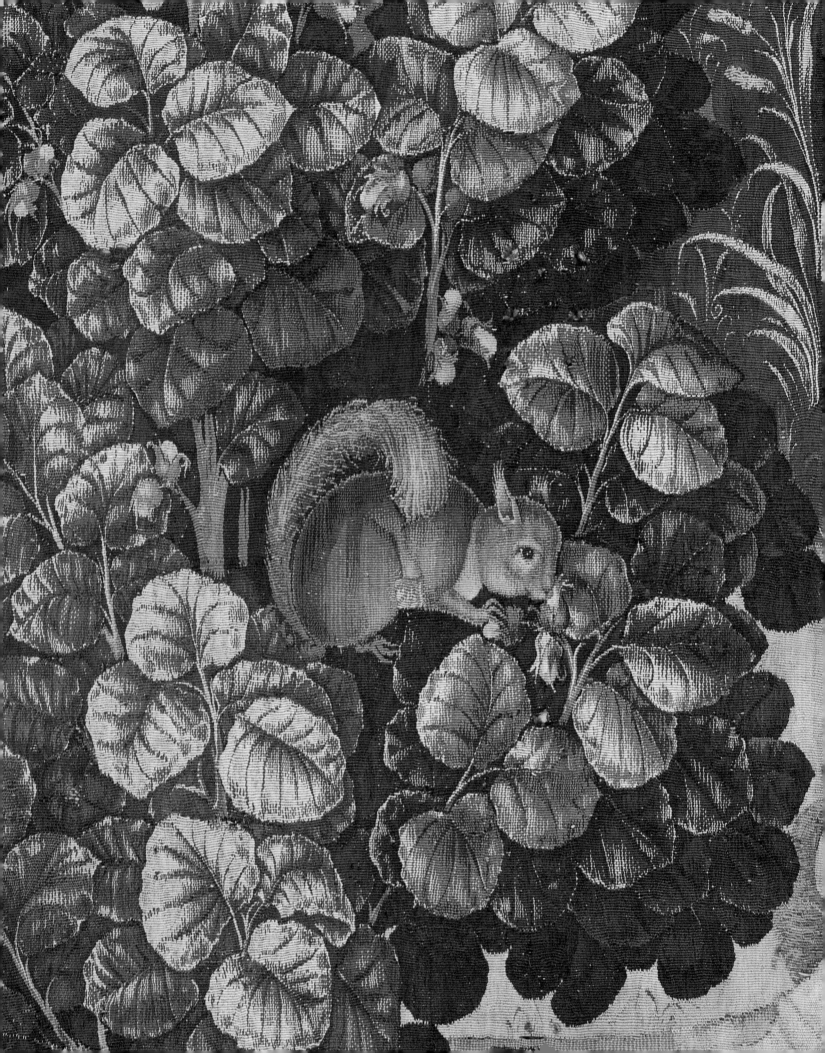

Squirrel. This charming detail from *The Hunt of the Unicorn* shows a squirrel perched in a hazelnut tree. The delicate ear tufts on this furry little creature enable us to identify it as a European red squirrel, a tree-dwelling species native to both Europe and Asia. The appearance of a squirrel in this, the sixth tapestry, in which the unicorn is killed, may have some symbolic value, for the squirrel has taken refuge above the earth from the danger posed by the hunters and dogs on the ground below. The hazelnut tree, which appears elsewhere in the tapestry series, also has meaning here; it was considered in medieval times to have the magical ability to regenerate if broken and thus could symbolize immortality or fidelity.

Squirrel Figurine. This delicate eighteenth-century Meissen figure was modeled by J. J. Kändler (German, 1706–75) in hard-paste porcelain. Squirrels, which are found throughout Europe, were valued for their fur, although this particular animal, like the European jay perched above, must have been admired by the artist for its delightful shape, especially the long, curling tail that echoes the rococo forms elsewhere in the piece. The word squirrel derives from two Greek words, *skia* meaning shadow and *oura* meaning tail, indicating that the ancients accurately observed the squirrel using its tail to shade it from the elements as well as its enemies.

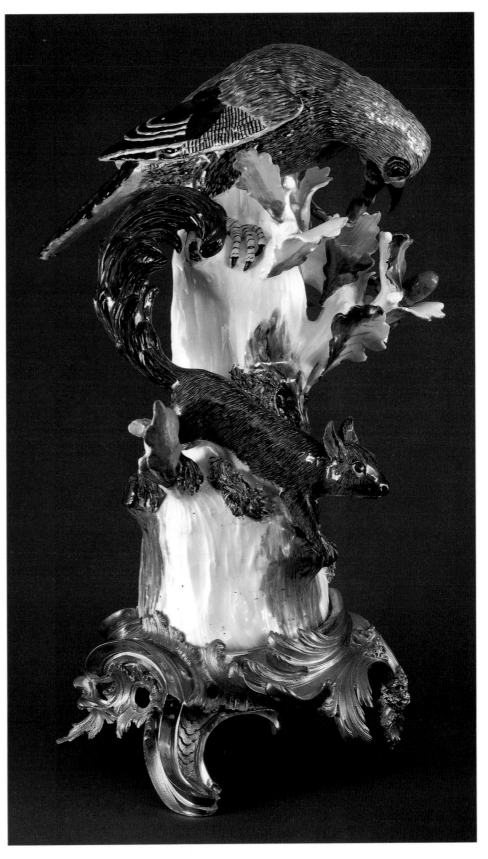

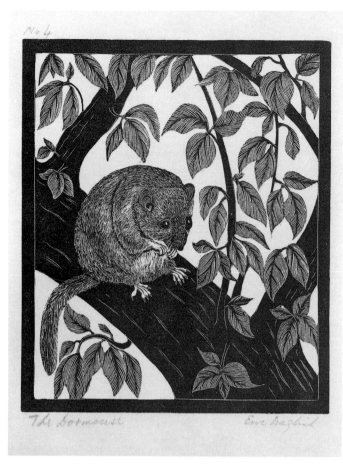

The Dormouse. The most familiar member of a family of small rodents found in the Old World is the common or hazel dormouse depicted in this woodblock print by Eric Daglish (British, 1894–1966). Nocturnal in habit, the dormouse may best be remembered as the guest who fell asleep during the Mad Hatter's tea party in *Alice in Wonderland.* Another species, aptly named the edible dormouse, becomes quite plump in preparation for its winter hibernation. Ancient Romans considered it a culinary delight.

Hudson's Bay Lemming. The oil painting below, by John Woodhouse Audubon (American, 1812–62), pictures one of the small rodent species found in the colder regions of North America. The lemming turns white in winter, like the animal on the left, and is thus more difficult for a predator to see against a snowy background. Following the completion of his monumental work on birds, John James Audubon (American, 1785–1851) published *The Viviparous Quadrupeds of North America.* Seventy-four of the 150 plates in the book were made from paintings by his younger son, John Woodhouse, including the one illustrated here.

Porcupines. The title of the painting opposite, made in 1914 by R. W. Chanler (American, 1872–1930), might well be "A Convention of Pincushions." The porcupine's long, sharp quills are loosely attached to its body and can be shed readily in any close encounter with an enemy. A series of minute barbs at the end of each quill ensures a painful and persistent bond and makes the quills especially difficult to remove. The sharpness of the quills and the distinctive black and white coloration of the animals— as well as the markings of the birch trees—obviously appealed strongly to the artist, who must have taken great pleasure in drawing the quills with a sharp point on the black painted surface.

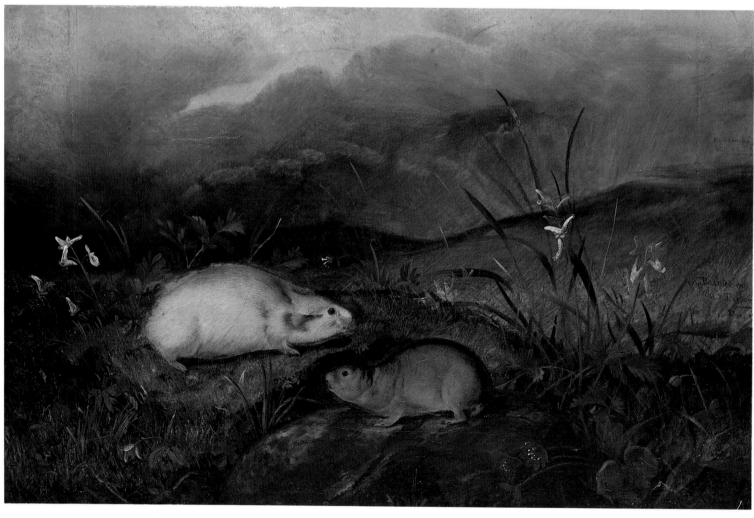

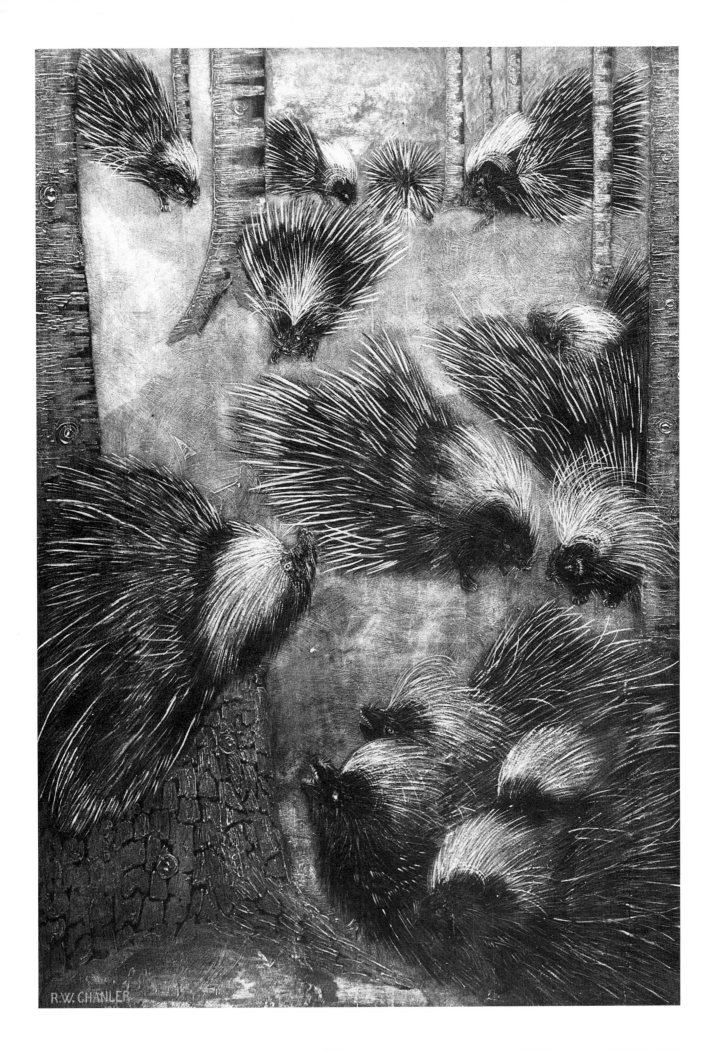

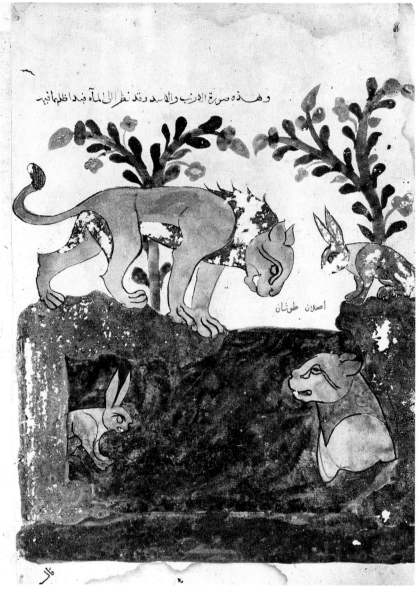

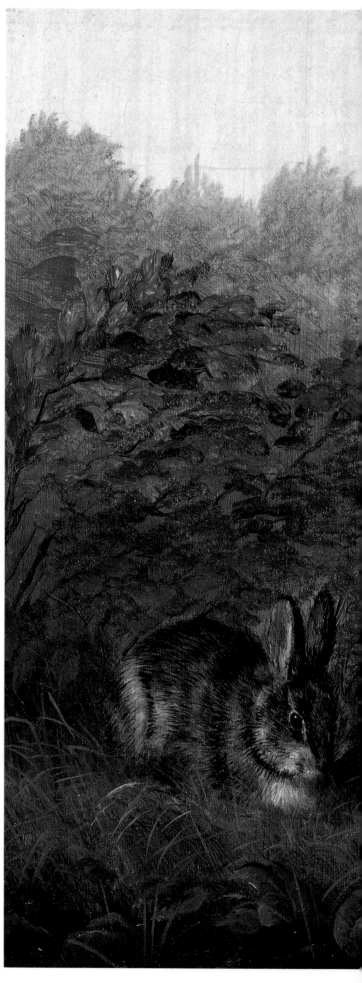

Kalila wa Dimna. Hares are among the most familiar animals in the world; with their relatives, the rabbits, they live on every continent except Antarctica. Both hares and rabbits have been hopping through legend and across the pages of books for centuries. While Aesop's hare was unable to win out over the slow, steady tortoise, the hares in this illustrated book of fables from sixteenth-century India look entirely capable of forcing these two lions into submission. Here the hares probably serve primarily as animal representations of human traits, as in Western art, in which hares have often symbolized lust, fertility, and—when chasing a knight—cowardice.

Rabbits on a Log. The group of rabbits in this oil painting by Arthur Fitzwilliam Tait (American, 1819–1905) has no symbolic connotation at all but is simply a depiction of wild animals in their natural habitat. This type of painting was popular in the nineteenth and early twentieth centuries. These rabbits are Eastern cottontails, the species that charms city dwellers in parks and plagues gardeners in the suburbs.

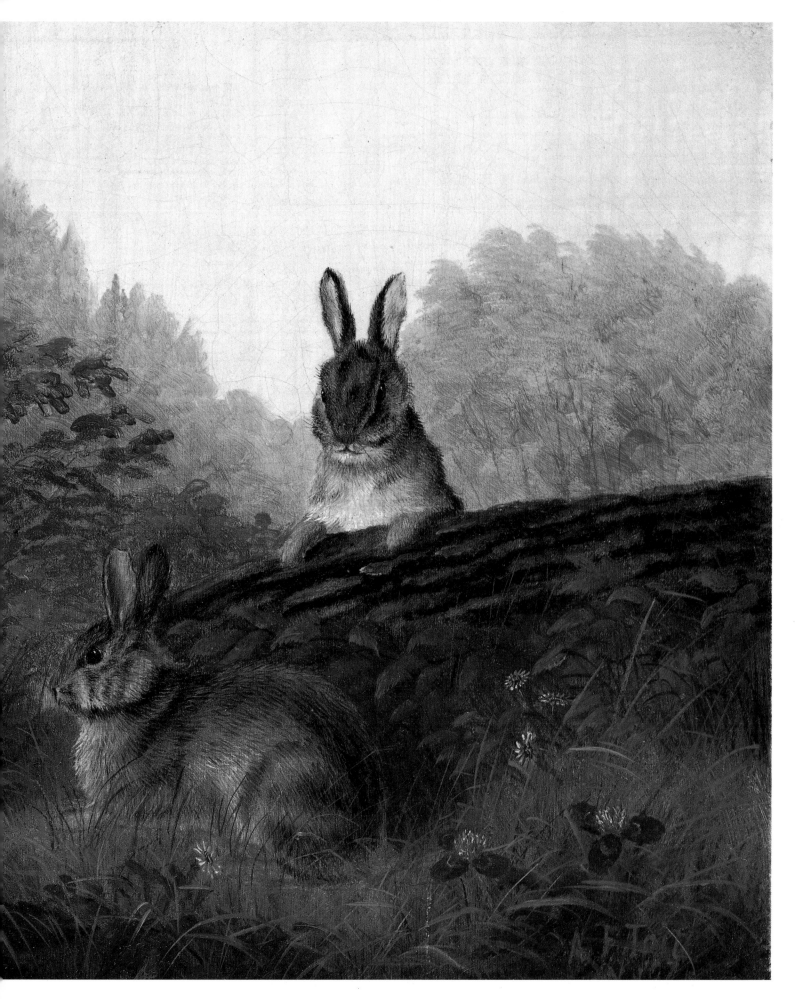

Perfume Vases. The two containers below left are shaped and marked like hares; they come from Corinth in Greece and date from the beginning of the sixth century B.C. Hares were frequently represented in Greek art, in hunting scenes or on objects such as these perfume vases, which were often made in animal shapes.

Snowbound. A cold, white winter landscape is the setting for a brown hare in the print (bottom right) by Eric Daglish. When deep snow covers the grains, seeds, and roots on which hares normally feed, they subsist on shrubs, twigs, and bark. Hares have longer legs than rabbits and are capable of running forty miles an hour for short distances; the snowshoe rabbit of the American West is, in fact, a hare, not a rabbit.

Rabbit Netsuke. The tiny ivory masterpiece below right was carved by one of Japan's outstanding netsuke artists of the nineteenth century, Ohara Mitsuhiro (1810–75). Although the animal's form has been simplified in this figurine, which is no more than one and a half inches in length, the basic characteristics have been retained in detail. The netsuke thus presents an appealingly lifelike rabbit.

Rabbit. The detail (opposite) from the second tapestry of *The Hunt of the Unicorn* shows a rabbit sitting in a field of flowers and grass. Its relatively short ears and legs suggest that it is the common wild rabbit of Europe, ancestor of more than sixty domestic breeds. One of several species of wild animals that appear in the tapestry series, the rabbit is especially appropriate here as a symbol of fertility, for the series may have been made as a wedding gift.

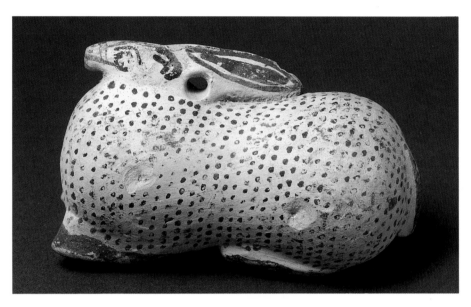

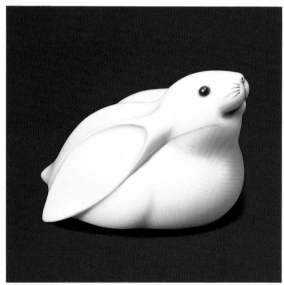

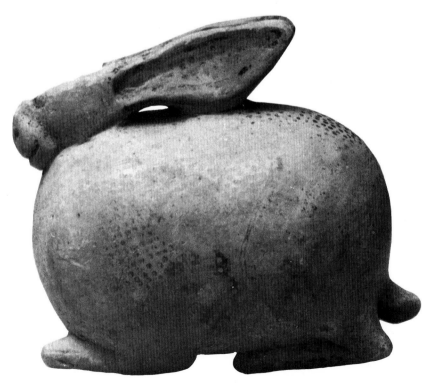

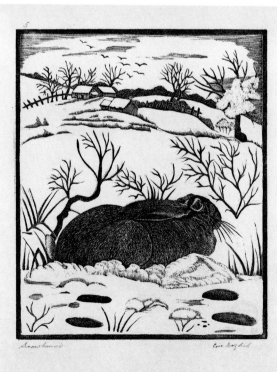

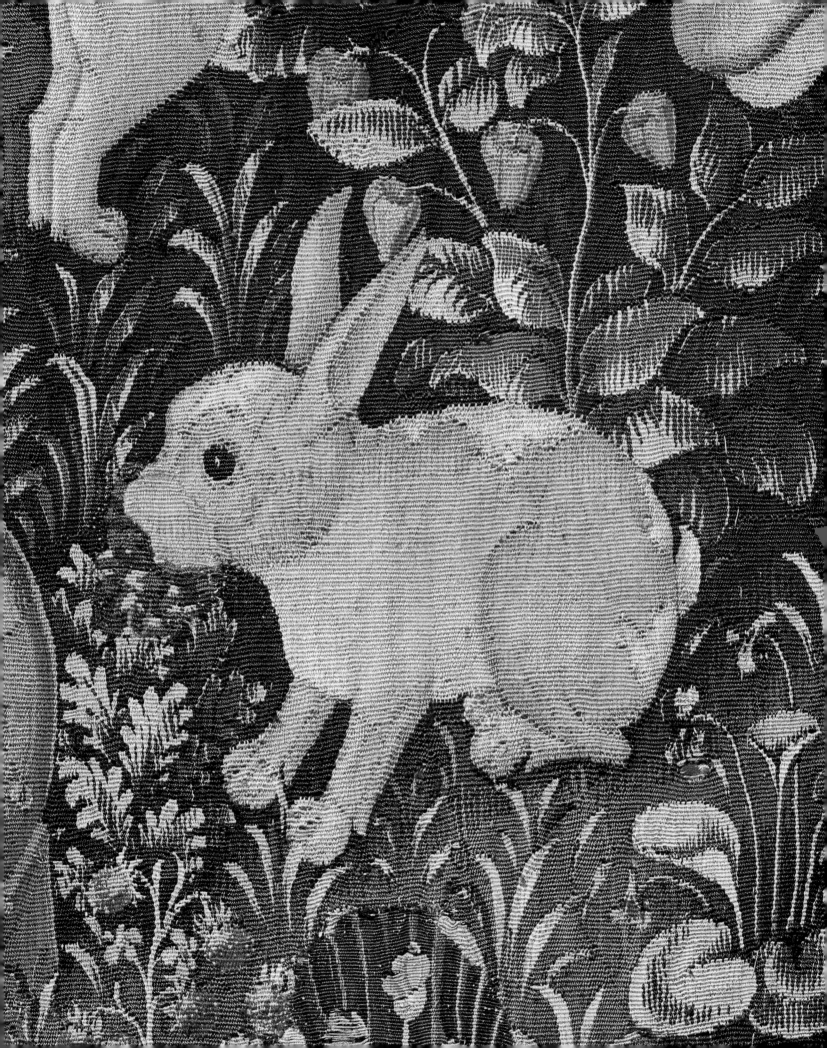

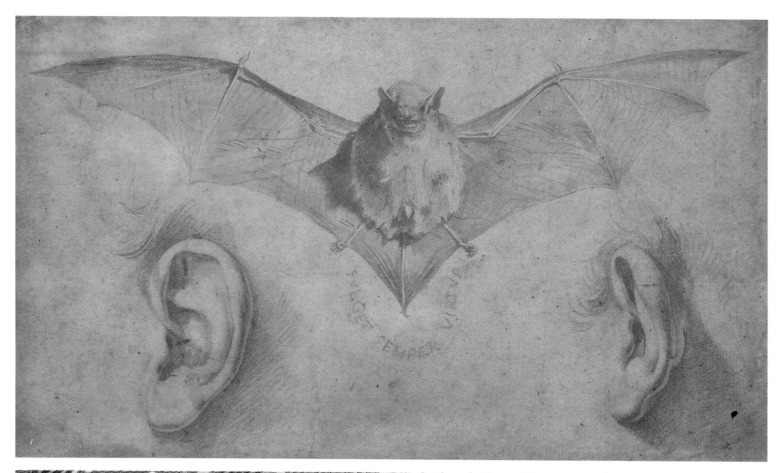

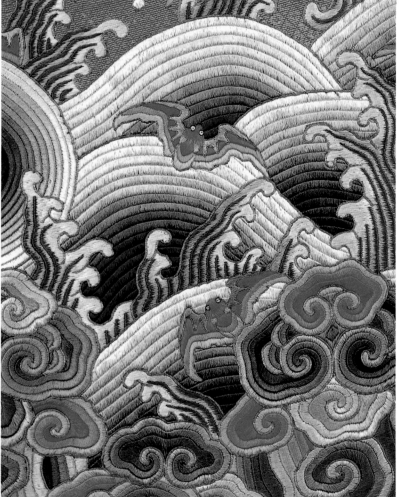

Studies of a Bat and Two Ears. In this superb red chalk and wash drawing by Jusepe de Ribera (Spanish, 1591–1652), the bat is executed in great detail to show the delicate structure of the animal's highly modified arm, hand, and leg bones, as well as the thin skin membrane that connects them to form its wings and tail. Even the soft body fur is clearly defined. This drawing is of special interest because a bat also figures on the coat of arms of Valencia, the region where Ribera was born. (Legend has it that a bat landed on the helmet of Aragon's King James I as he fought to regain Valencia from the Moors in 1503.) Beneath our bat appears a motto: "Virtue Shines Forever." The human ears, drawn in red chalk, were studies made for an etching produced in 1622 and have no connection with the bat; Ribera may not even have known that the reason bats fly so well in the dark is that they have extraordinarily sensitive ears.

Imperial Robe. Vividly depicted in red, blue, and green, two bats in glossy silk-float stitches flutter like butterflies above the ocean waves in this detail from the border of a Chinese emperor's robe made in the eighteenth century. Fashioned of red-silk gauze embroidered all over with golden-yellow silk, the garment was designed to be worn on formal occasions at court. Bats are auspicious symbols in China and signify longevity, wealth, love of virtue, a natural death, and happiness.

Bat Medallion Robe. This exquisite Manchu woman's court robe of golden satin is embroidered with stem stitches of satin and silk in a variety of tones softened by centuries of interment in the tomb of Prince Kuo (1697–1738) and his consorts. It was worn for birthdays, anniversaries, and other happy occasions. Although bats are often feared and even abhorred in the West, they are symbols of happiness in China because the characters representing "happiness" and "bat" are both pronounced "fu."

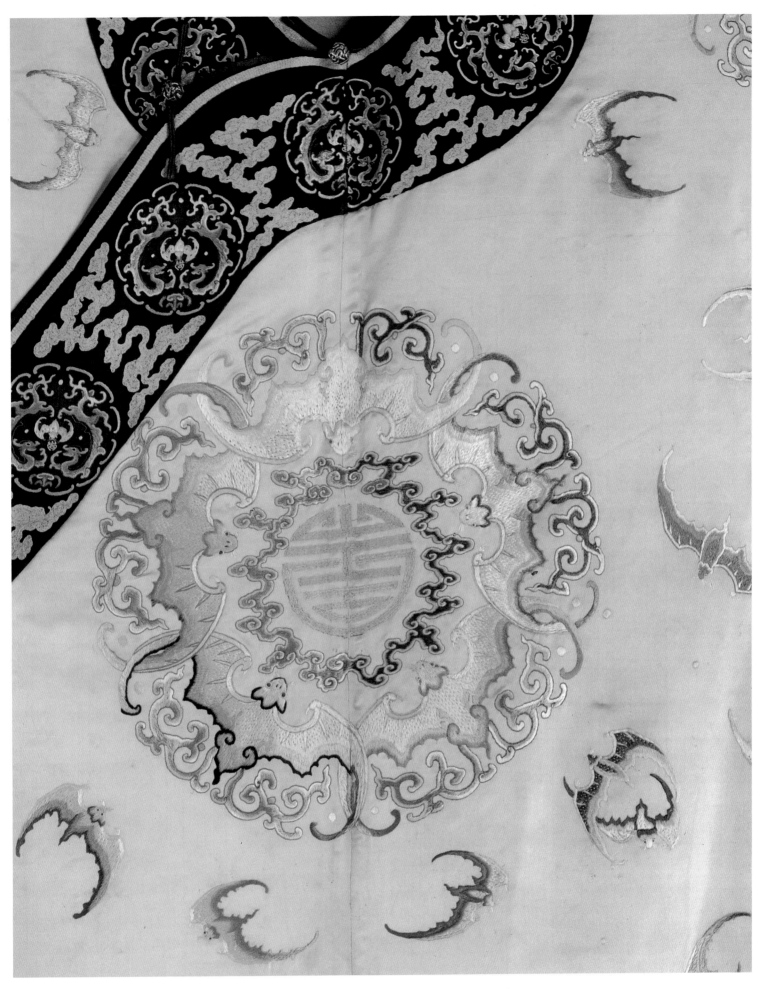

Monkey. This conté-crayon drawing by Georges Seurat (French, 1859–91) was made as a study for the figure of a monkey that appears in the foreground of Seurat's most famous painting, *Sunday Afternoon on the Island of La Grande Jatte,* depicting Parisians enjoying themselves on an island in the Seine. This graceful little animal is probably a capuchin monkey, native to the New World tropics but once popular as a household pet and organ-grinder's companion.

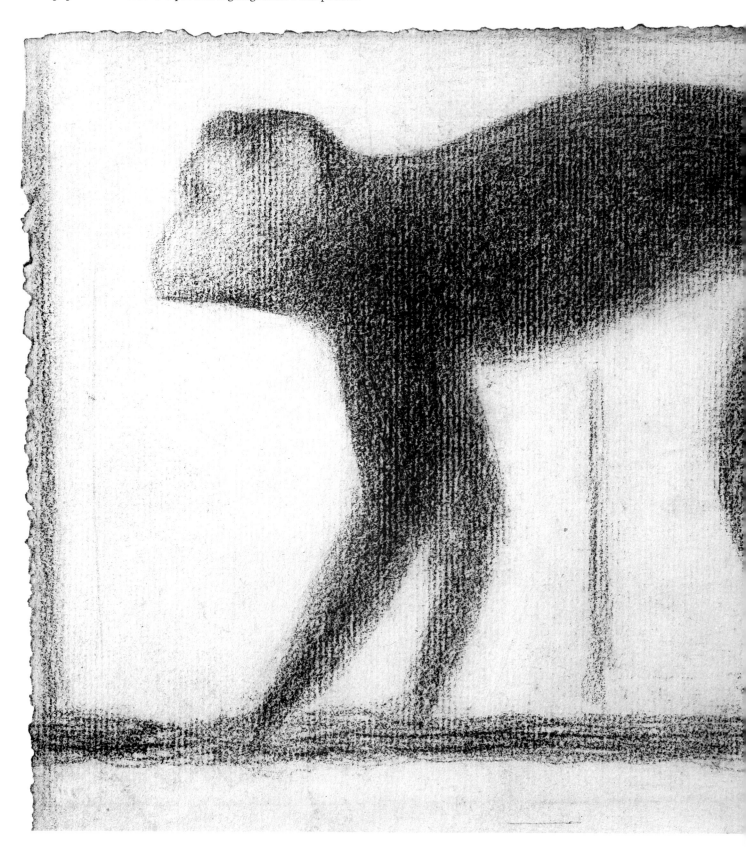

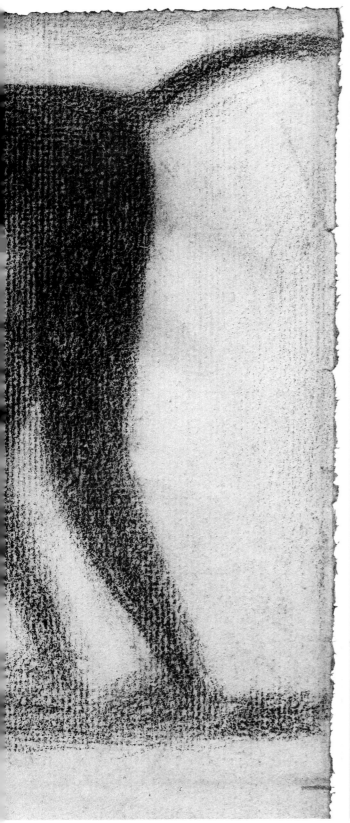

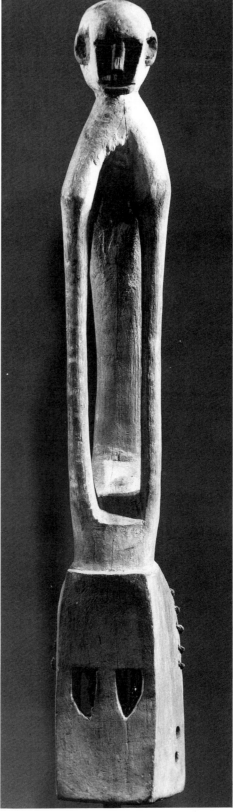

Monkey Mask. The Dogon people of Mali in West Africa wear these carved wooden headpieces at memorial ceremonies because they believe the masks will help to remove the spirit of the deceased from the village. The masks are also used to help drive out the spirits of animals killed in the hunt.

Egyptian Baboon. Sometimes called "dog-faced" monkeys, baboons were highly regarded by the ancient Egyptians, who associated them with Thoth, the god of wisdom and learning. The statue below, most likely a votive offering, depicts a Hamadryas baboon, a species common in the savannahs south of Egypt.

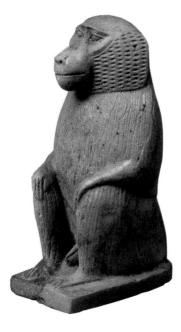

Monkey and Fruit. The monkey on the opposite page appears in the lower right corner of a painting by Melchior d'Hondecoeter (Dutch, 1636–95); the full painting is reproduced on page 104. Best known for his skill in painting ornamental fowl, d'Hondecoeter was equally adept in representing mammals. His rendering of the soft pelage of the vervet monkey, or guenon, a native of southern and eastern Africa, contrasts sharply with the metallic sheen of the peacock's train.

Three Monkeys. A contented pair of Japanese macaques share a quiet moment with their baby in this section (right) from a pair of six-panel screens painted in the style of Mori Sōsen (Japanese, 1747–1821), who was noted for his animal paintings, particularly those of monkeys. Here the mother grooms her infant while the male attends closely, looking as aloof and dignified as he can manage.

Monkey Cup. Vases in the ancient world were often made in the shape of animals, and a number of them are illustrated in this book. In the example below, however, the animal—a monkey—has been adapted to fit the standard shape of a cup, a clay kantharos made in Cyprus during the first half of the fifth century B.C.

OVERLEAF: **Monkey Screen.** A pair of white-handed gibbons is stopped in action as they swing gracefully through the branches on this six-panel screen by the Japanese artist Suizan Miki (1891–1957). Executed in ink on silvered paper with a black wooden border, the screen is one of a pair painted by the artist. Native to the tropics of Southeast Asia, gibbons are the most arboreal of all the anthropoid, or manlike, apes. They rarely come to the ground, but when they do they walk in an upright fashion and use their long arms for balance. In the treetops they are capable of incredible acrobatic feats, often leaping thirty feet or more as they move from one branch to another.

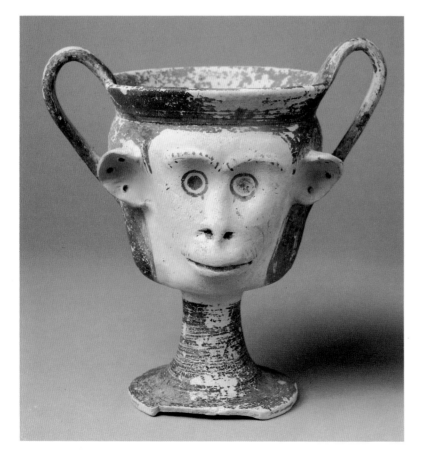

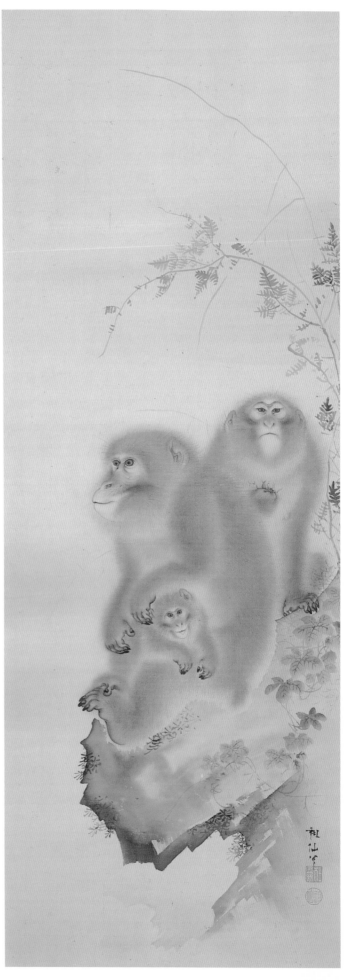

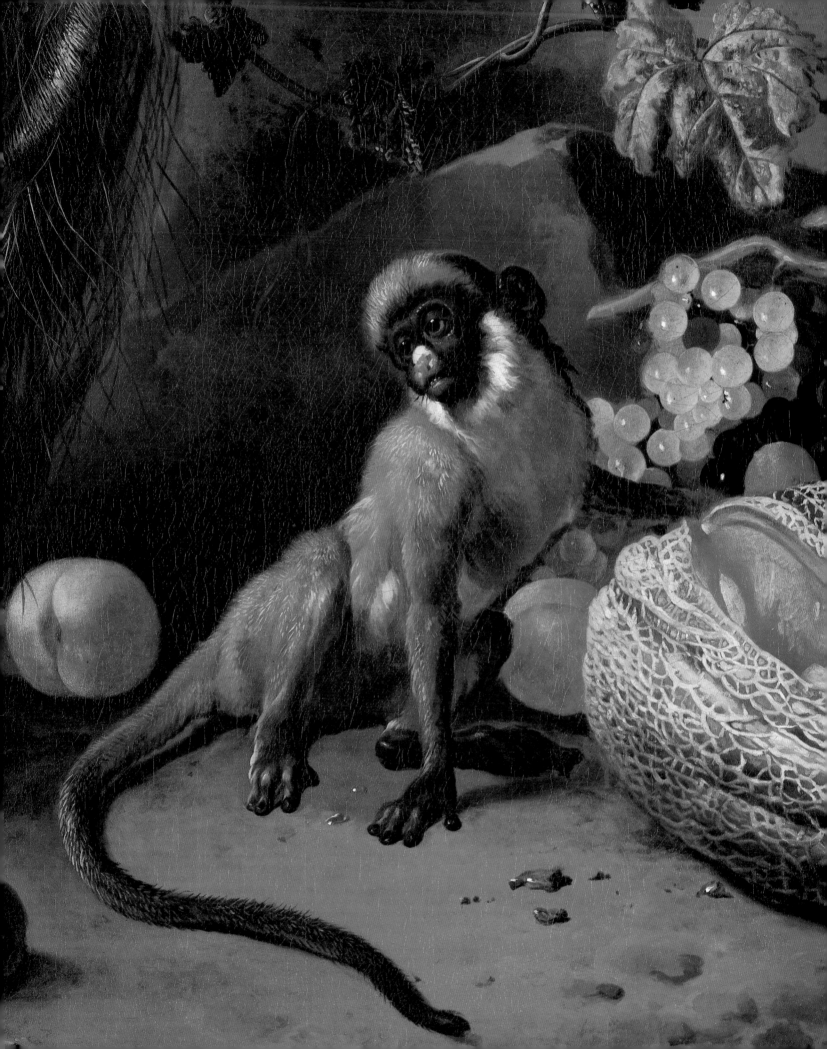

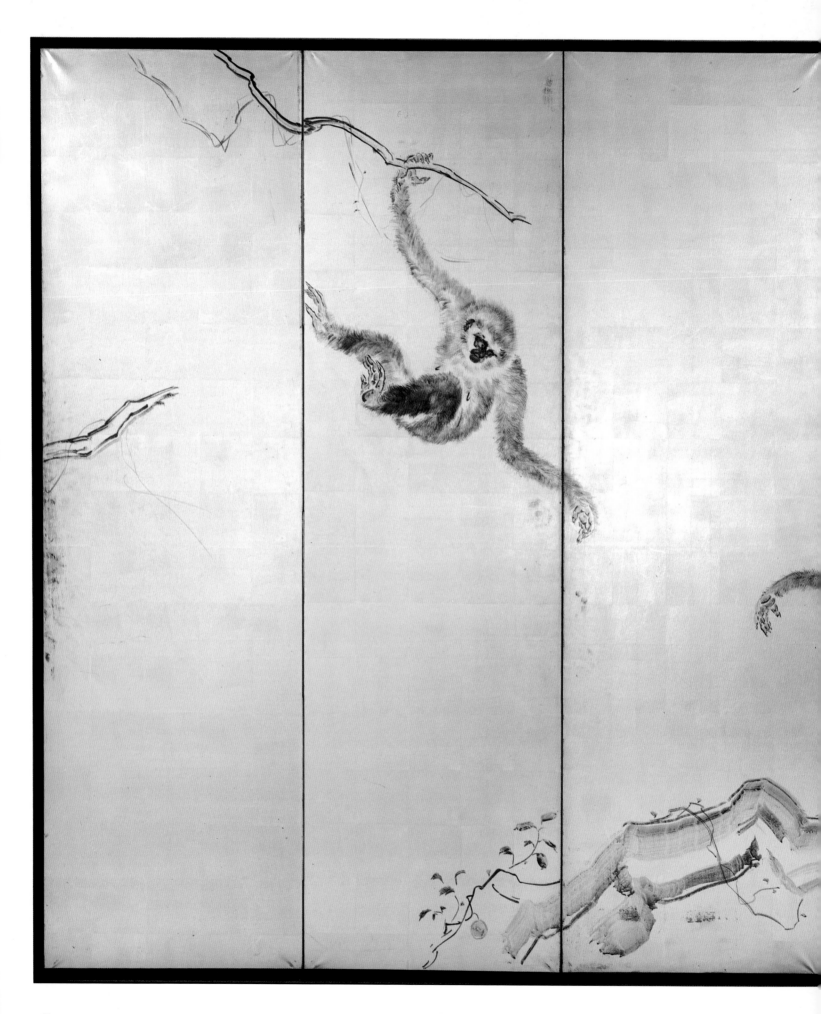

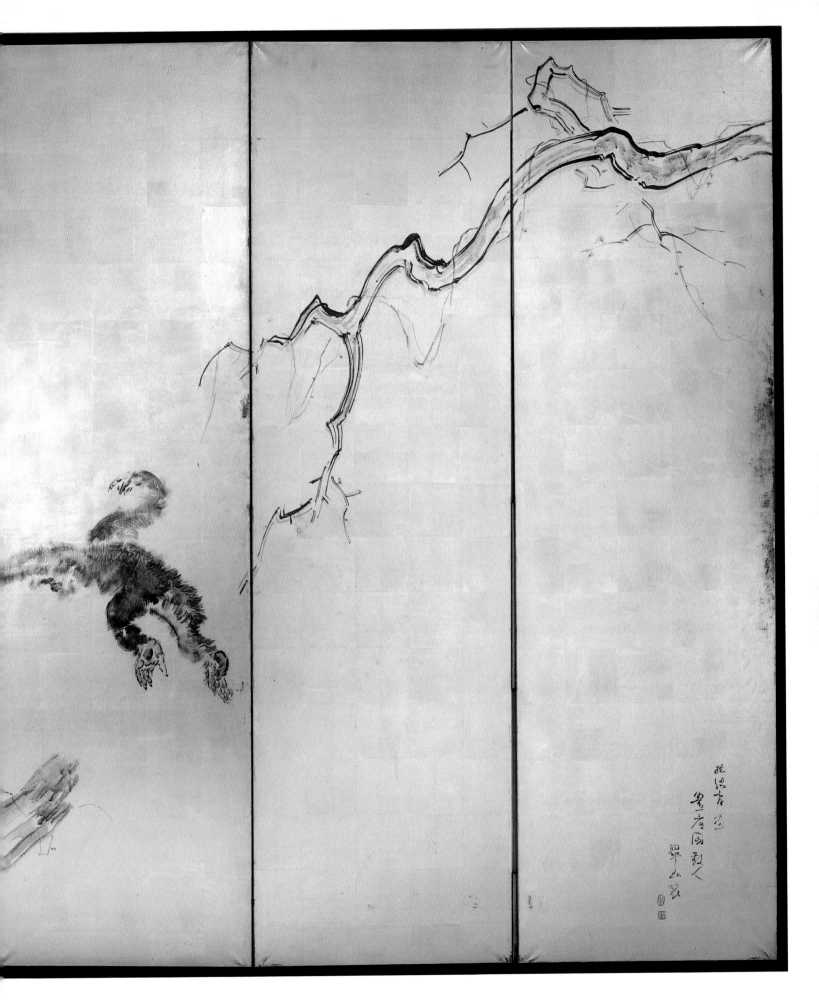

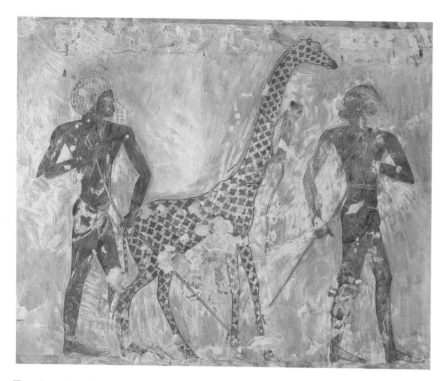

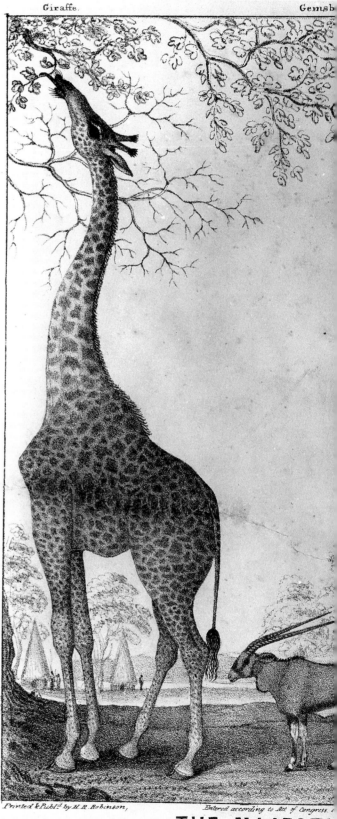

Egyptian Giraffe. Wall paintings in the tombs of politically powerful Egyptians frequently show scenes of foreigners paying tribute in processions of products, plants, and animals of their native countries. In this facsimile of a wall painting from the tomb of Rekhmira dating to about 1475 B.C., we can see two Nubians leading a giraffe by ropes around his forelegs. The artist clearly had an accurate eye for detail as well as a sense of humor, for he has shown a green monkey climbing up the giraffe's neck, much as they are known to do in nature to steal rides from one group of trees to another.

The Majestic and Graceful Giraffes, or Cameleopards. In this procession, created over three thousand years later than the Egyptian example above to advertise a circus in nineteenth-century America, the giraffe is once more the center of attention as an exotic curiosity. Again attended by a native African, the giraffes—also called cameleopards, a verbal hybrid—are accompanied (left to right) by a gemsbok, an eland, a gazelle, and two Nubian goats. Tallest of all living mammals, male giraffes may reach a height of eighteen feet; curiously enough, however, they have the same number of neck bones as all other mammals, including humans.

Printed & Publd by H.R.Robinson,   Entered according to Act of Congress,

THE MAJESTI
With some RARE ANIMALS of the GAZELLE SPECIES, from a drawing made
hibition of the kind in the WORLD. These animals were captured in the wilds of S
We hereby certify that the above is a correct and faithful representation of the

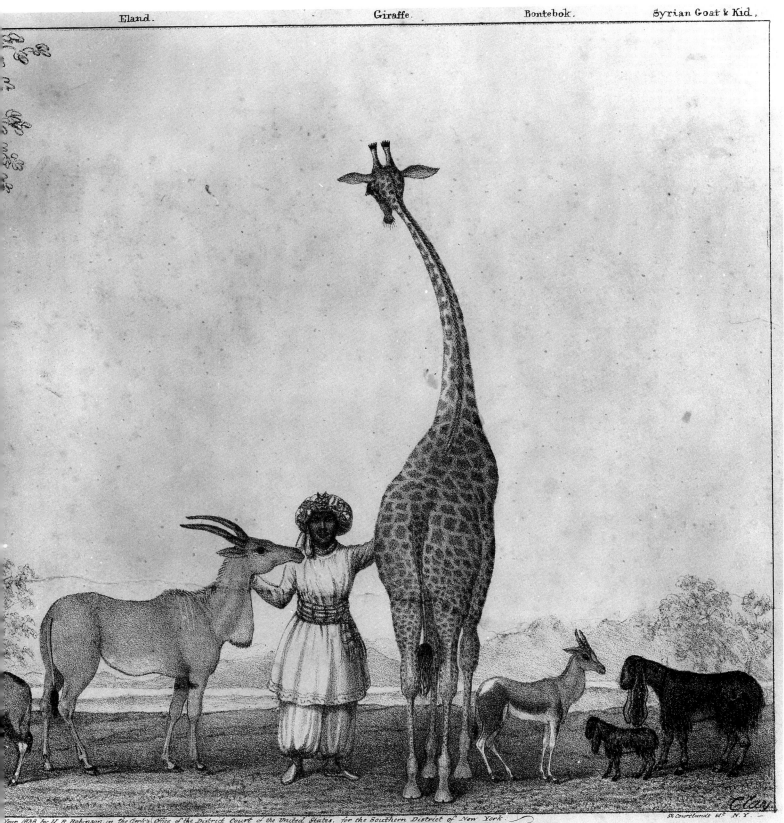

Year 1838, by H. R. Robinson, in the Clerk's Office of the District Court of the United States, for the Southern District of New York.   56 Courtlandt St. N. Y.

AND GRACEFUL GIRAFFES, OR CAMELEOPARDS

e beautiful pavillion, Nᵒ 509, Broadway, where hundreds daily resort to gaze with delight upon these elegant quadrupeds, the first ever seen in America and, with one exception, the only ex-
Africa, by Mr Clayton, and were recently imported, at an immense expenditure, by Messrs Welch, Macomber and Weeks.
ls, and was made under our immediate inspection.

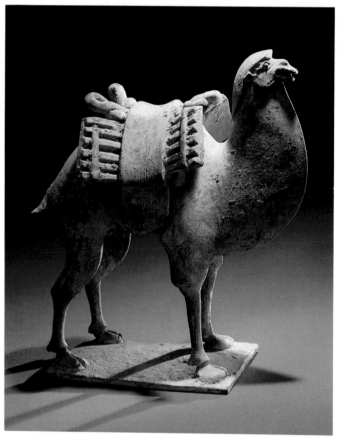

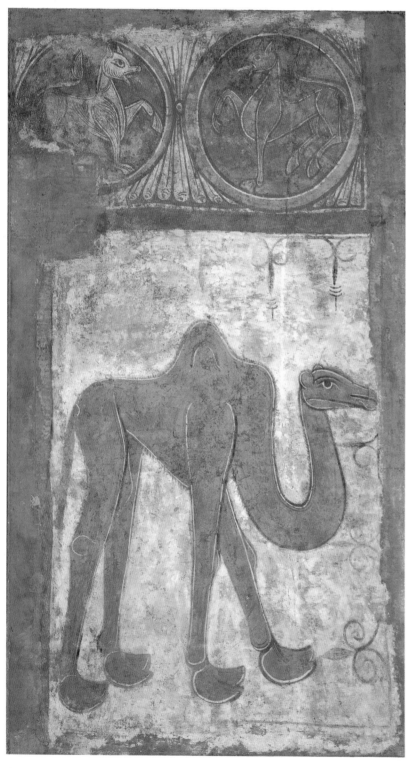

Bactrian Camel. The Bactrian camel served as the delivery truck on the Central Asian trade routes, carrying bolts of silk and other exotic goods traded intermittently between China and countries as far away as Rome. The routes were most active from the time of Christ until the fourteenth century when the Ming dynasty closed China's doors to the West. This earthenware camel was molded during the Northern Wei dynasty in the sixth century; these picturesque beasts later proliferated as grave figures during the great Golden Age of the T'ang dynasty (618–906), when they were brightly glazed and shown off in spectacular funeral processions.

Camel Bowl. In spite of their length of service to humans, camels and dromedaries still retain a wild spirit and resist complete domestication. Nevertheless, they are most often depicted as beasts of burden, like these dromedaries that decorate an Islamic plate from the tenth century. Since no riders are to be seen, these animals, fitted with canopied saddles or litters, may have a symbolic or ceremonial function rather than a practical one.

Dromedary Fresco. The Spanish painting at the left dates from the twelfth century and comes from the Church of San Bandelio in Berlanga, Spain. The camel here is native to the hot, dry regions of Africa and Asia. The thick footpads, somewhat exaggerated in this painting, act to protect their feet from the hot sands of the desert, while the thick eyelashes, as well as hair in the ears and nostrils, help keep out the blowing sand. Two spirited horses, perhaps of North African origin like the dromedary, prance in the panels above.

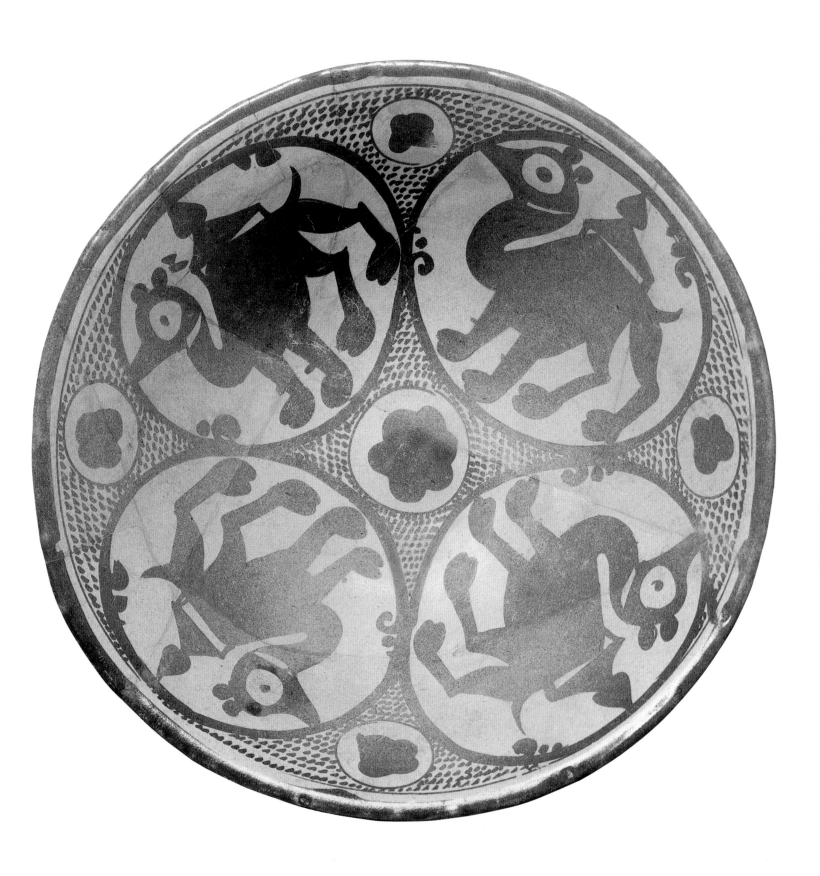

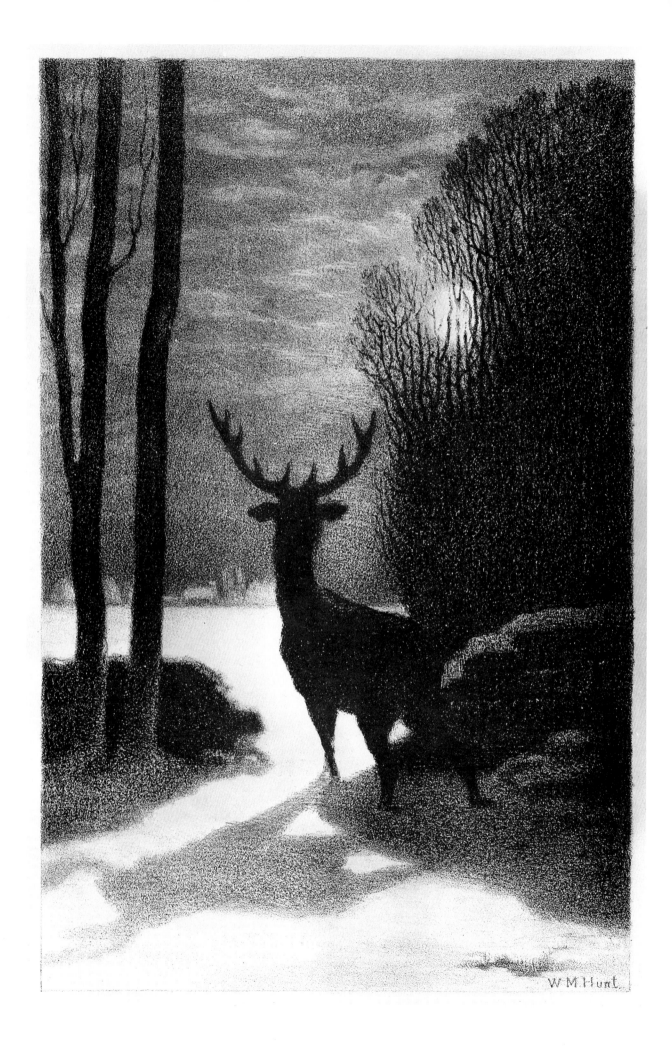

The Stag in Winter. In the stillness of a winter's night, the moonlight silhouettes an eight-point buck and casts its shadow on the snow. This impressive sight is handsomely depicted in the black-and-white lithograph (opposite) by William Morris Hunt (American, 1824–79). Hunt, originally intending to be a sculptor, went as a young man to Paris, where he studied painting and was influenced by members of the Barbizon School. He was very interested in the effects of light, as can be seen here, and was one of the earliest American Impressionists.

Two Stags Running. Sir Edwin Henry Landseer (British, 1802–73) was an extremely popular animal painter and a favorite of Queen Victoria and Prince Albert. He was best known for his paintings of horses, dogs, and stags, to which he often gave human attributes in sentimental portrayals, but he was also recognized as a fine draftsman and a keen observer of nature. In this quickly rendered sketch in brown wash (right), Landseer has used a minimum of brushwork to capture two red deer stags in full flight.

Dish with Large Deer. During the fifteenth century some of the finest glazed pottery in the world was made in Spain. Known as Valencian lusterware, after the region where it was produced, it was made with a unique glazing process that simulated the rich sheen of precious metals. Valencian lusterware pieces usually bore a design on the back as well as on the front; the figure on the back of this plate from the Cloisters Collection is a highly stylized stag—probably a red deer, the most common species of deer to be found in Europe, where it was a favorite quarry of hunters.

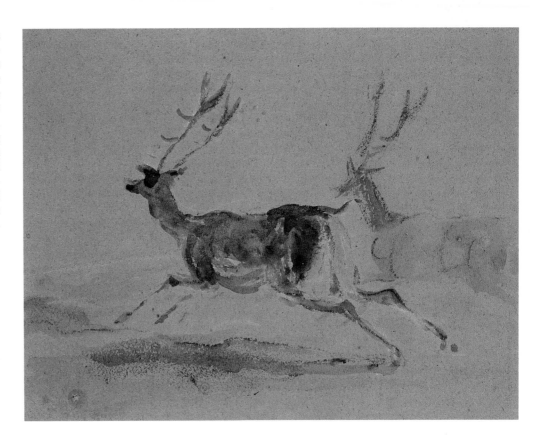

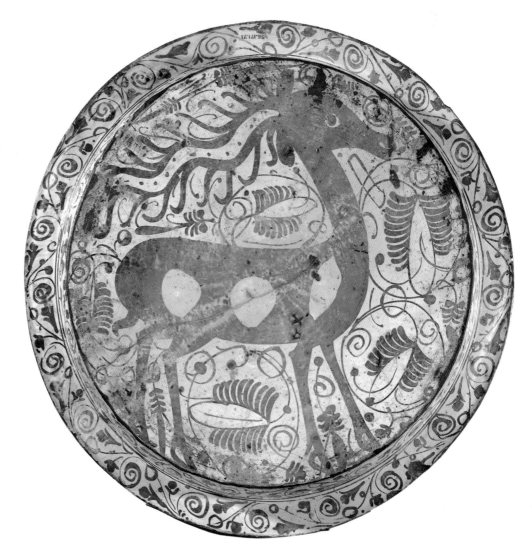

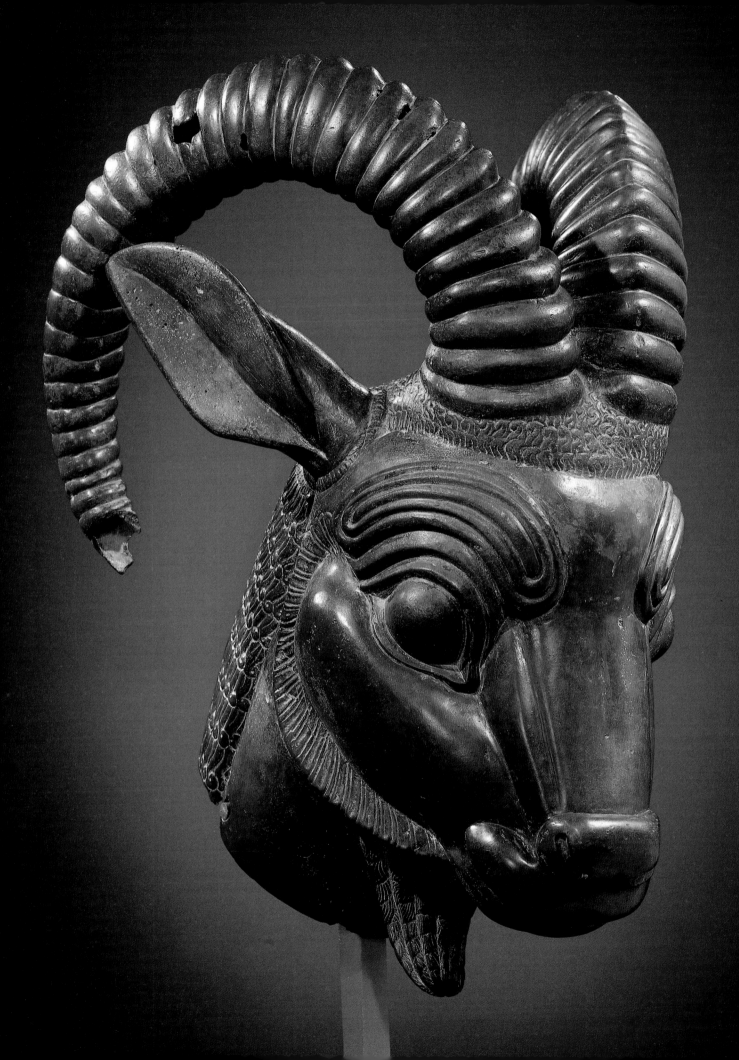

Head of a Horned Animal. This strikingly beautiful bronze sculpture of the Achaemenid period in Iran (sixth–fourth century B.C.) was cast in five separate pieces—the ears, horns, and head—that were then joined together. The head might be identified as that of an ibex, which is native to mountainous regions in Europe and Asia, but it is more likely a composite animal, incorporating the horns of a sheep and the beard of a goat.

Irish Mountain Goat. Startled, a goat looks back from its perch on a rocky pinnacle to detect the presence of an enemy. The sculptor of the granite and aluminum work below left, John Bernard Flannagan (American, 1895–1942), was highly regarded for his direct stone carving of birds and mammals, and he has successfully preserved the natural feeling and texture of the stone in this work without sacrificing the animal's agile grace. There are no truly wild goats of any variety in Ireland, but Flannagan may have been inspired to make this sculpture during one of his two trips to that country during the 1930s.

Antelope Headdresses. Worn by the Bamana people of Mali in West Africa during a ceremonial dance, these wooden antelope figures of the nineteenth and twentieth centuries would be attached to the basketry caps of the performers. The dance would be held in honor of *Chi wara*, a mythical being who taught mankind the secrets of agriculture by scratching the earth with his claws.

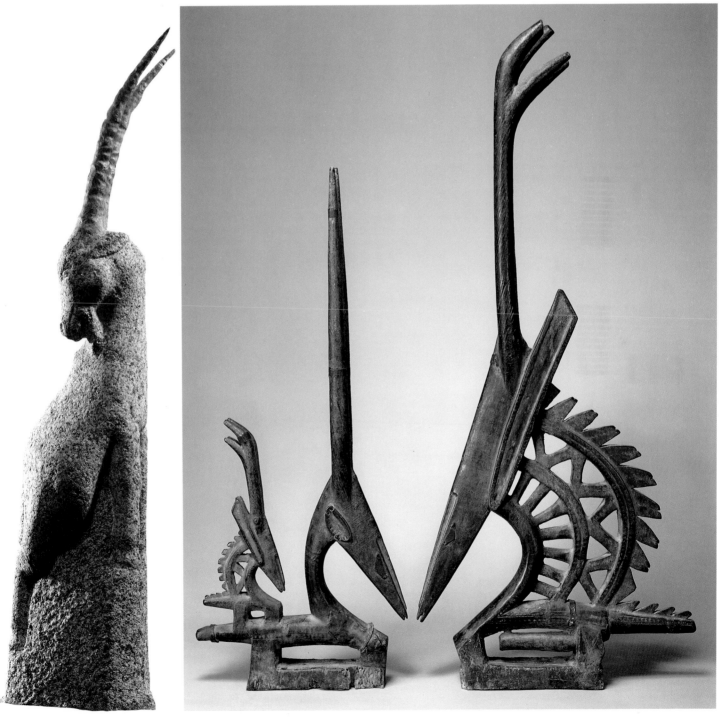

A Gazelle. An unknown Lombard artist of the early fifteenth century produced the beautiful drawing below by using silverpoint and pen and ink and adding colors with a brush. The animal may be a female Persian gazelle, the only species of gazelle in which males alone have horns, and possibly a specimen brought to Europe from Africa as a new addition to a private menagerie. Like other European artists of the time, this one may have been commissioned to record the animal's appearance or he may simply have been attracted to the appealing creature for its own qualities.

Egyptian Gazelle. Fashioned from a simple piece of ivory and mounted on a wooden base, the graceful figure of a gazelle on the opposite page (upper left) is an Egyptian sculpture carved during the New Kingdom, toward the end of Dynasty 18 (ca. 1379–1362 B.C.). The fact that the horns and ears are missing detracts not at all from the charm of this delicate-looking animal, which can, nonetheless, run at

speeds of up to forty miles an hour on the open grasslands where it lives.

Gazelle Cup. The ancient gold vessel illustrated on the opposite page was made by a craftsman around 1000 B.C. in the region southwest of the Caspian Sea. This cup has four gazelles, rendered in relief, walking around its surface. Their heads, which are executed in the round, were modeled separately and added to the cup; the horns and ears were added to the heads.

Nilgai. The painting opposite, probably by Mansur, the master court painter for Shah Jahan, fifth Mughal emperor of India, pictures a nilgai, or "blue bull," of India, the largest of all Asiatic antelopes. The animal shown here is a male; females are brown and lack the short horns. This splendidly painted example is a leaf from the Kevorkian *Shah Jahan Album,* a collection of Mughal paintings of the seventeenth century.

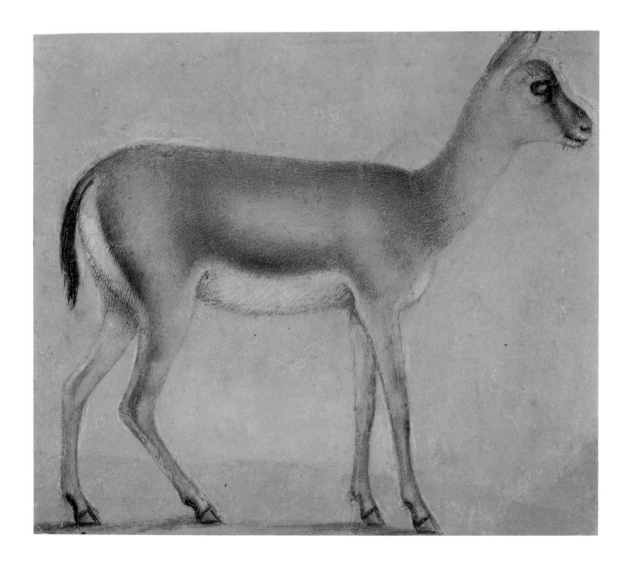

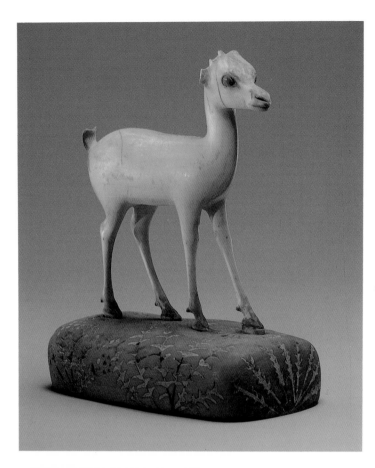

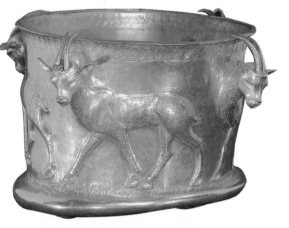

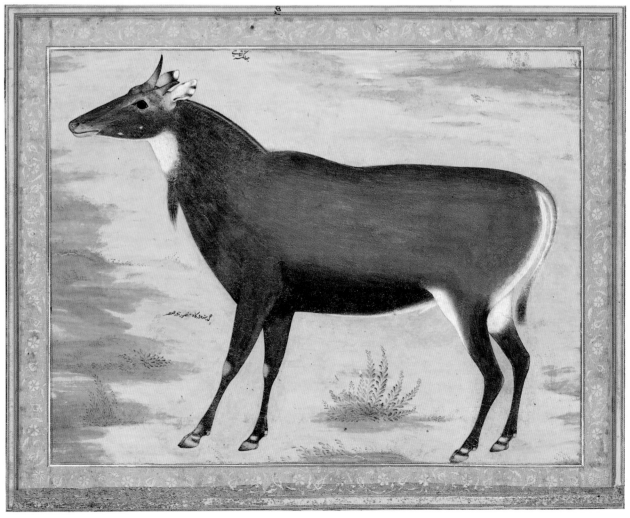

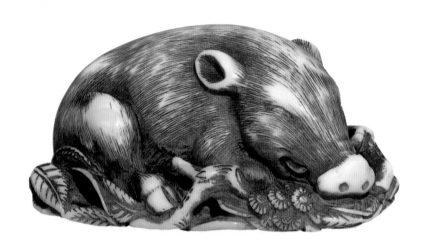

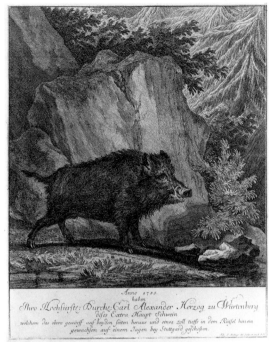

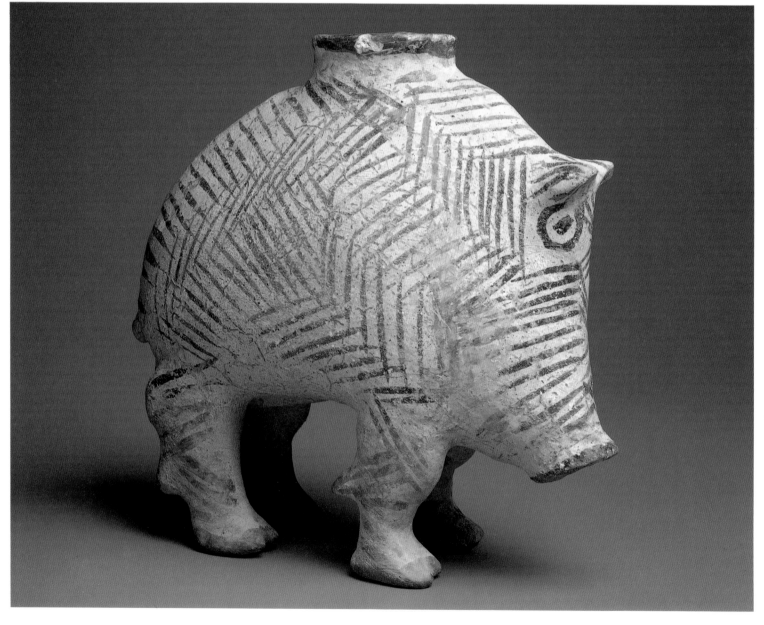

Boar Netsuke. On the opposite page (above left) is a charming eighteenth-century Japanese ivory carving of a boar sleeping on a bed of ferns and boughs. Although little more than two inches long, the animal's body is clearly defined in every detail. The flat, rubbery snout, typical of all pigs, is useful for finding food on the forest floor.

Wild Pig. Thickset, hairy, and powerful, the wild boar pictured in the engraving opposite (above right), dated 1735, by the German artist Johann Elias Ridinger is just as dangerous as it looks. Because wild boar are cunning and savage when cornered, hunting of them has been considered big-game sport since prehistoric times. Native to Europe and Asia, wild boars were introduced into North America for the purpose of hunting and are still wild in some areas.

Boar-shaped Vessel. Opposite, below, is a ceramic vessel fashioned as a standing wild boar by a potter working about 2900 B.C. in south-western Iran. Vessels made in the shape of animals, like this one, were probably used in religious ceremonies. The bold zigzag body pattern represents the boar's long, wirelike bristles.

Boar Krater. In black-figured Greek vase paintings of the early sixth century B.C., friezes of animals, such as fallow deer, panthers, lions, and boars, often appeared beneath the main picture. The choice of two boars as the primary image on this handsome krater comes out of this tradition, but it is the achievement of Sophilos, to whom the painting is attributed, to have made something wonderful out of what was usually considered secondary decoration. Although boars will fight fiercely with each other, using their sharp tusks as weapons, the artist most likely did not intend to present a scene of combat here.

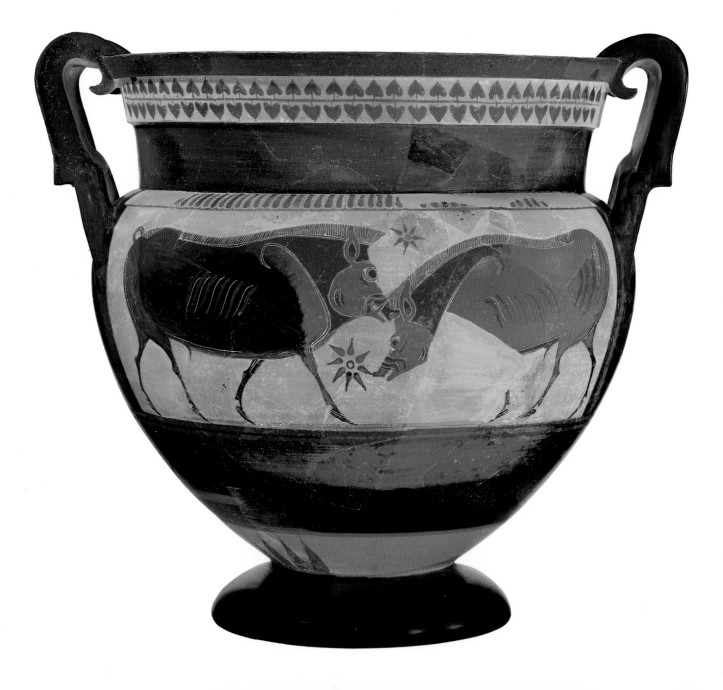

Two Kangaroos. As a source of food and material for clothing and tools, kangaroos have always been of great importance to Australian aborigines and often the subjects of their art. In this bark painting, the kangaroos' form is silhouetted and its vital organs visible in the "X-ray" style typical of the Northern Territory. Bark paintings were used in hunting and fertility rituals as well as for lining the interiors of temporary shelters.

Water Buffalo. The massive body structure and innate power of an animal that may stand more than five feet tall at the shoulder and weigh over 1,500 pounds are clearly seen in the sculpture in nephrite from China reproduced on the opposite page. Originally native to the hot lowlands and swamps of India, Sri Lanka, and the Malay Peninsula, the water buffalo has been for years a patient beast of burden in East Asian countries, particularly where wet rice is grown.

Egyptian Hippopotamus. Ancient Egyptians feared hippopotamuses as symbols of destructive forces in nature and made likenesses of them as amulets to control and ward off such power. This blue-glazed hippo figurine (known in the Museum as "William") was found at Meir in the tomb of the Steward Senbi, who lived during Dynasty 12 (ca. 1991–1786 B.C.). The designs on William's back represent some of the varieties of plants found in the habitat of the hippopotamus, which at the time this figurine was made included Egypt as well as areas south of the Sahara.

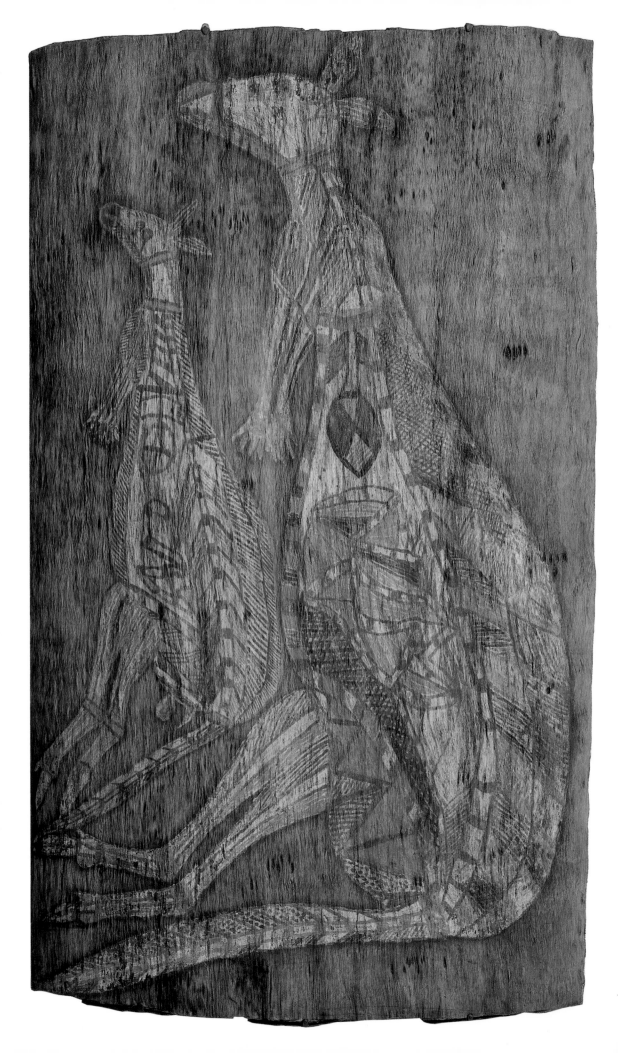

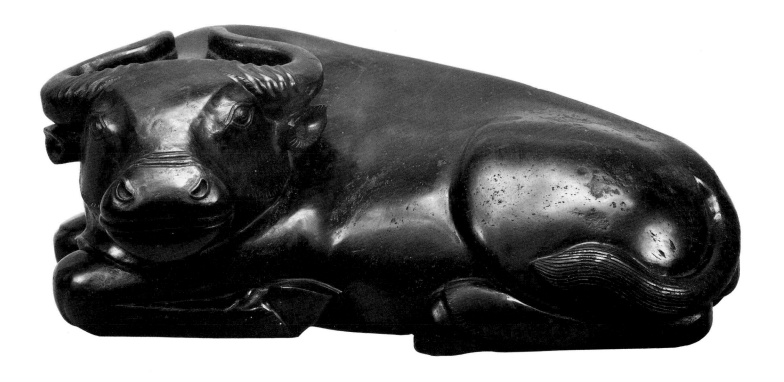

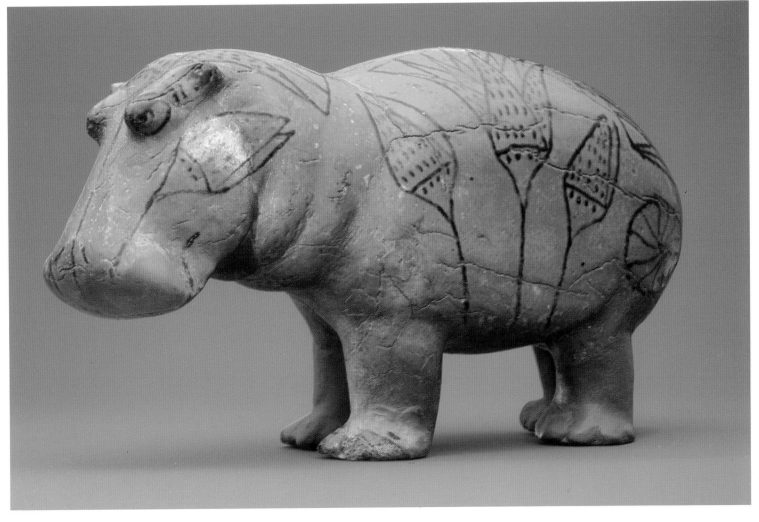

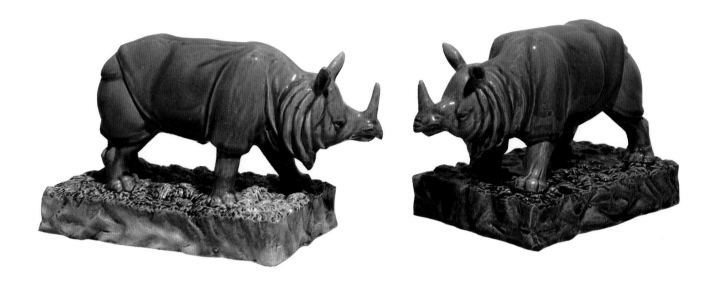

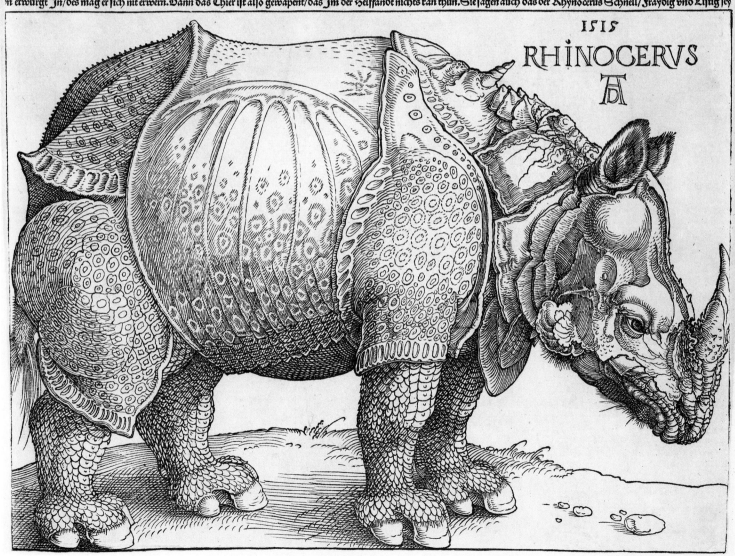

Nach Christus gepurt.1513. Jar. Adi.j. May. Hat man dem großmechtigen Kunig von Portugall Emanuell gen Lysabona pracht auß India/ein sollich lebendig Thier. Das nennen si Rhinocerus. Das ist hye mit aller seiner gestalt Abcondertfet. Es hat ein farb wie ein gespreckelte Schildtkrot. Vnd ist von dicken Schalen vberlegt fast fest. Vnd ist in der gröfs als der Helfand aber nydertrechtiger von paynen/vnd fast werhafftig. Es hat ein scharff starck Horn voun auff der nasen/Das begyndt es albeg zu werzen wo es bey staynen ist. Das dosig Thier ist des Helf hantz todt feyndt. Der Helffandt furcht es fast vbel/dann wo es In ankumbt/so laufft Im das Thier mit dem kopff zwischen dye fordern payn/vnd reyst den Helffandt vnden am pauch auf vnnd erwürgt In/des mag er sich nit erwern. Dann das Thier ist also gewapent/das Im der Helffandt nichts kan thün. Sie sagen auch das der Rhynocerus Schnell/ Fraydig vnd Listig sey

1515
RHINOCERVS
AD

Rhinoceros. Although Albrecht Dürer (German, 1471–1528) never actually saw an Indian rhinoceros himself but based his woodcut on a sketch and description sent to Nuremberg from Lisbon, it was considered the finest picture of a rhinoceros for more than two hundred years after its creation in 1515, and it remains one of the most famous animal portraits ever made. Dürer was often drawn to animal subjects, and it is not surprising that he would have been intrigued by the arrival in Europe of an exotic beast from Asia. Armor was still worn in Europe at this time, which may have influenced contemporary perception of the rhinoceros's hide as a suit of metal plates and chain mail. But even with the knightly treatment and the addition of a tiny, imaginary horn to the animal's withers, it is still a very good rhinoceros.

Rhinoceros Figurines. These two pottery figures, modelled by the British artist Ralph Wood and glazed with color during the eighteenth century, bear a strong resemblance to Dürer's rhinoceros portrait created over two centuries earlier.

Rhinoceros Platter. The English Chelsea platter below, made in the mid-eighteenth century, truly reproduces Dürer's rhinoceros, here surrounded with foliage, flowers, butterflies, and other insects that the animal would never have met in its native Asian habitat.

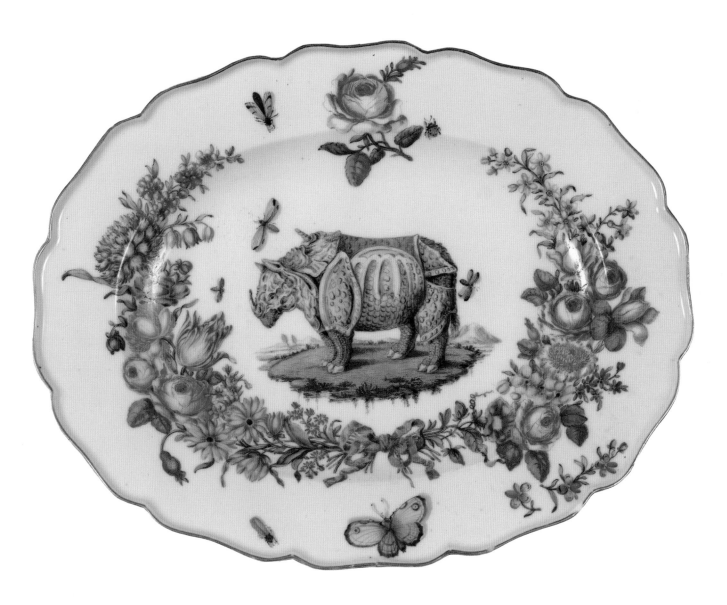

Asian Elephants. As the largest of all living land creatures and one of the most popular attractions in circuses and zoos, elephants need little introduction. There are two species, one from Asia and the other from Africa; the animals in the prints on these two pages are all Asian, a species once found throughout much of tropical Asia but now reduced to small, scattered groups increasingly threatened with extinction due to loss of natural habitat. The two large prints (below and at lower right) are engraved plates from a book produced by the painter, printmaker, and writer Jean-Pierre Houel (French, 1735–1813), who traveled widely during the late eighteenth century and produced a number of volumes on natural history. In the plate below, Houel shows the correct way to depict the characteristics of the head in different positions, and he has clearly defined typical features of the Asian species: a large head with a bulbous crown, small triangular ears, and a single fingerlike extension on the tip of the trunk. The plate on the opposite page shows two females with a baby elephant, one of them the mother—perhaps the exhausted one on the left!— and the other another cow in the same herd. At birth elephants weigh about 200 pounds but they grow steadily, and a full-grown male like the one in the engraving (opposite, top) by the Italian artist Stefano della Bella (1610–64) may tip the scales at more than six tons.

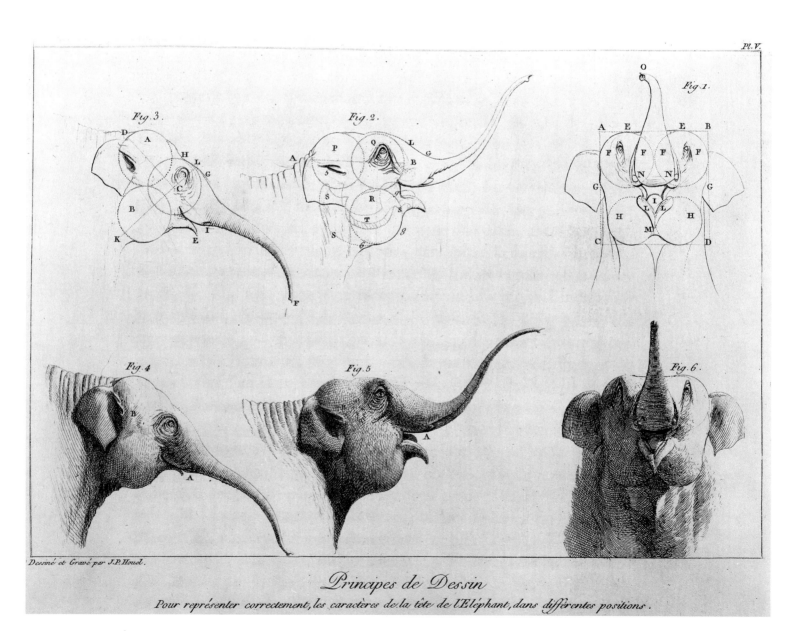

Principes de Dessin

Pour représenter correctement, les caractères de la tête de l'Eléphant, dans différentes positions.

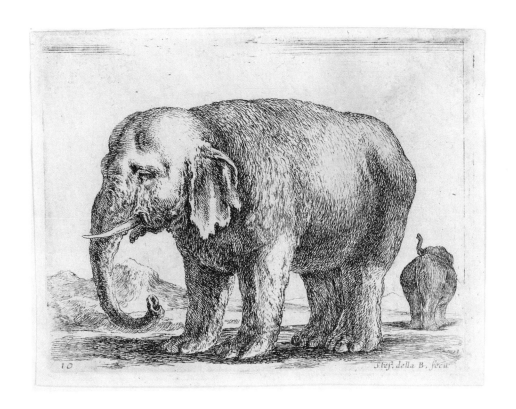

Pl. XVIII.

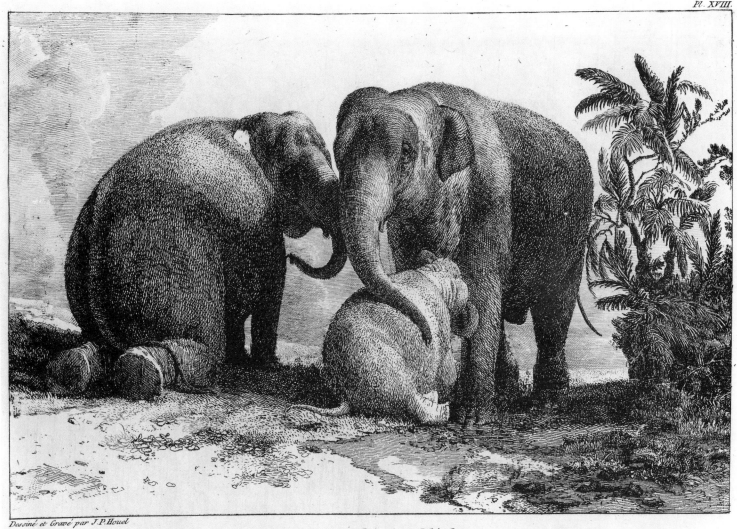

Dessiné et Gravé par J.P.Houel

Allaitement du petit Eléphant.

Chinese Elephant. In China elephants represent strength, wisdom, power, and energy. Albino, or white, elephants are considered by Buddhists to be the holiest of beasts because, in one of his prior incarnations, the future Buddha appeared as one with no less than six tusks. According to another legend, it was a white elephant that came to Maya in a dream and entered her womb as the future Buddha. Long the favorite mount and weapon of South Asian monarchs, elephants came to signify universal sovereignty, both temporal and spiritual, and have been a popular motif in the arts of all East Asian countries since the spread of Buddhism from India. Here one is embroidered in silk and metal thread with peacock feathers on a Buddhist priest's robe of the reign of the K'ang-hsi Emperor during the Ch'ing dynasty (1644–1912).

Senegalese Elephant. Even in this small bronze statue, the big-eared, heavily tusked African elephant is an impressive animal. A male may weigh seven tons and can run at speeds above twenty miles an hour for short distances; although smaller, African females may also carry fairly heavy tusks. Because of their size and strength, elephants have no natural enemies, except for humans, who have hunted them for sport and ivory throughout recorded history. The artist who has so successfully captured the power of the elephant here is one of the most famous animal artists, or *animaliers,* of the nineteenth century, Antoine-Louis Barye (French, 1796–1875). Barye's intimate knowledge of animal anatomy and behavior is clearly demonstrated. He once told Auguste Rodin, who studied with him briefly, that he modeled "from the bone up."

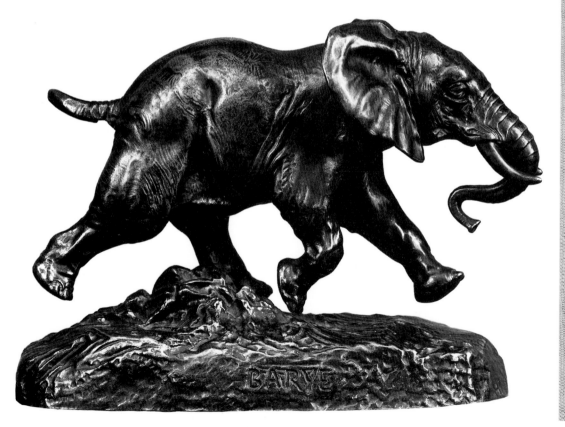

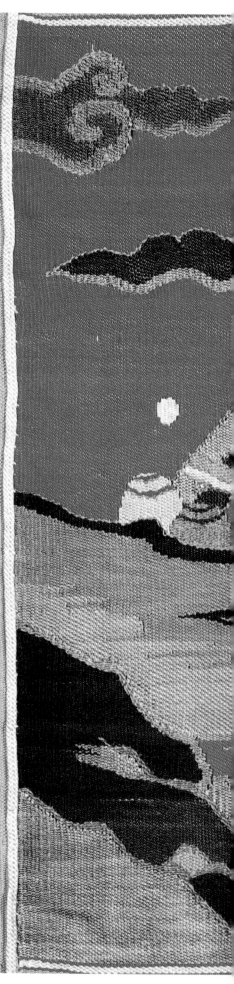

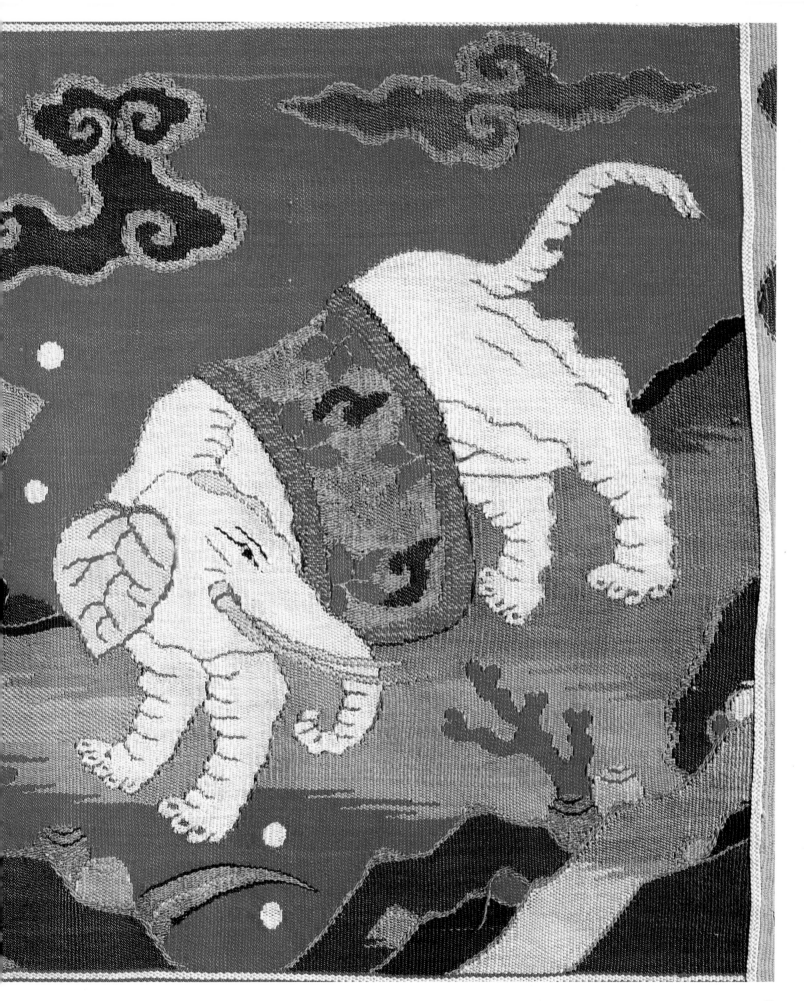

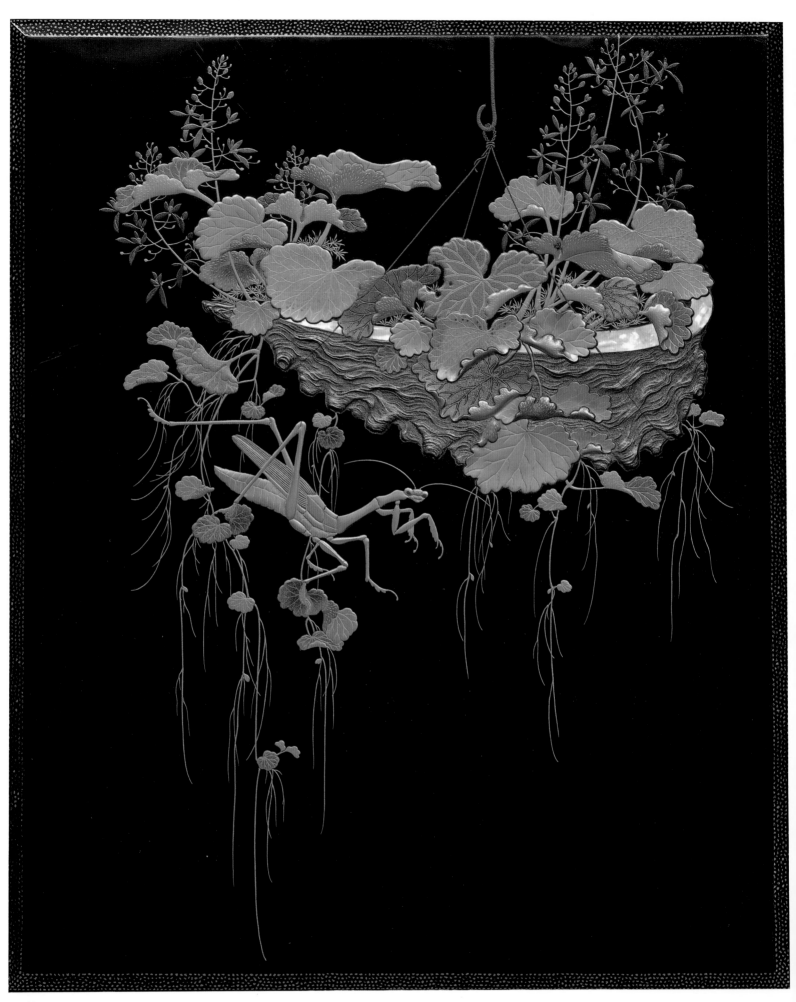

Praying Mantis. Hidden in the foliage of a hanging plant, a praying mantis lurks in ambush for any insect that might come its way. The word "praying" refers to the position in which this insect holds its forelegs, but it might well be spelled "preying," for the mantis is a voracious hunter that will, if the opportunity presents itself, devour its mate or young with great relish. The mantis, leaves, and flowers on the opposite page are pictured in a detail from a nineteenth-century Japanese writing-paper box, which was painted with lacquer and decorated with gold, pewter, and abalone shell. Successive layers of lacquer and gold were applied to the surface and then carved, shaped, and polished in a unique method developed by the Japanese to add greater dimension to the picture.

Insect Study. It has been estimated that about nine-tenths of all the animals on earth are insects. Well over half a million species have been described to date, and this may represent only one-tenth of the actual total. The painting illustrated below shows the variety to be found among insects. A watercolor on vellum, it is attributed to Georg (Joris) Hoefnagel (Flemish, 1542–1600) or his son Jacob (1575–1630), who made a number of studies of animals, flowers, and insects. Surrounded by moths, butterflies, a dragonfly, and other species, a huge stag beetle appears to be clutching the decorative border around the Latin word for black. An inscription at the bottom of the sheet is from Psalm 104: ". . . who maketh the clouds his chariot: who walketh upon the wings of the wind." Sharp eyes will note an alien among the group, just below the beetle's right wing: this eight-legged creature is a spider, which is an arachnid and not a true insect.

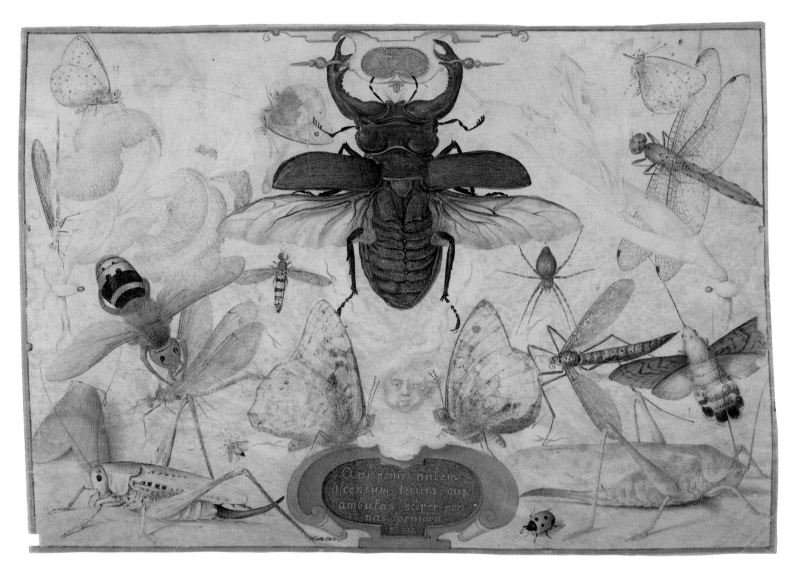

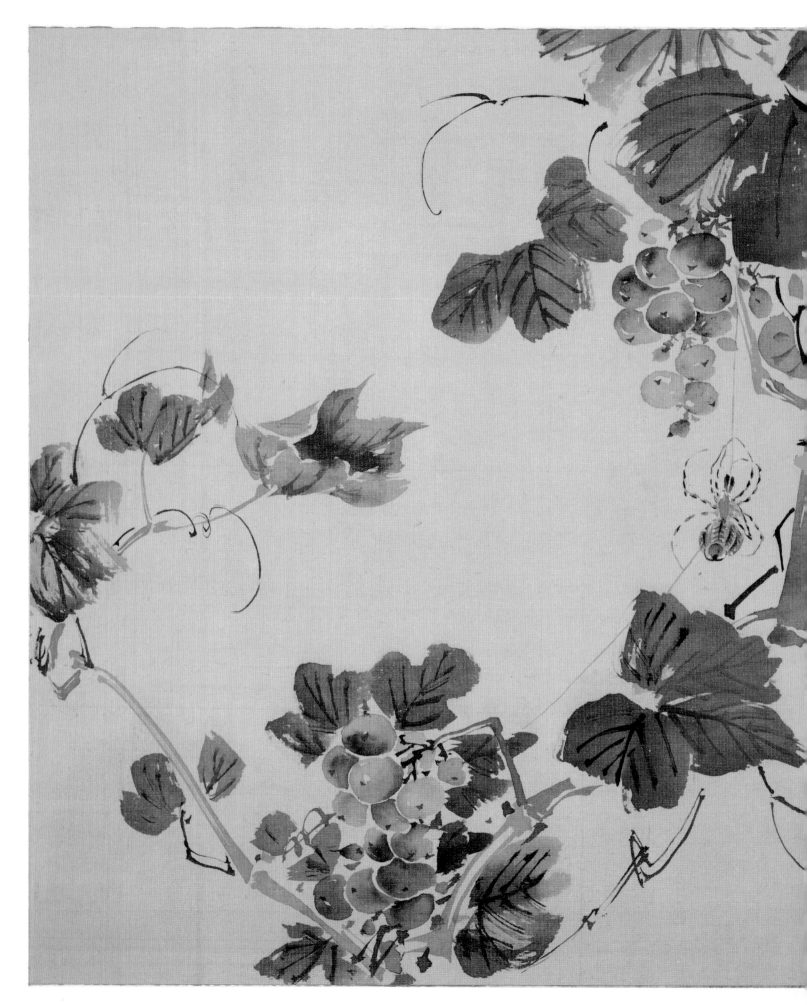

Japanese Spider. A combination silk factory, tightrope walker, and engineer, the spider spins its own thread, walks the high wire with ease, and constructs intricate structures for trapping its food. In this painting by the Japanese artist Katei (1830–1901), one of several leaves in an album of flower and bird paintings, a spider is beginning to erect its fragile-looking web between the branches of a fruit tree. Spider silk is, in fact, a very tough, fibrous protein, which may be stretched to one-fourth its normal length before breaking; some species produce a silk that is the strongest natural fiber known.

Beetle Watch. There are more than 250,000 species of beetles alone, more than the total number of all other animal species outside the insect world. Within the beetle group, there are 30,000 kinds of scarab beetles, which are similar in appearance to the gold beetle shown here with a watch set in its back, a nineteenth-century Swiss creation. The ancient Egyptians held one of the scarabs, which they called Taurt, sacred, as an incarnation of the sun; the European watchmaker who devised this handsome timepiece probably intended no particular meaning here beyond the attractive and clever use of movable beetle wings as a watch cover, though the ephemeral nature of an insect's life would make it an appropriate subject for a clock.

Crayfish Pendant. Precolumbian objects often took or incorporated animal forms, and works produced by the Chiriqui people of western Panama were no exception. They used alligators, armadillos, birds, monkeys, and many other animals in their pottery, stone carvings, and cast-gold objects, such as the pendant illustrated at the bottom of the page.

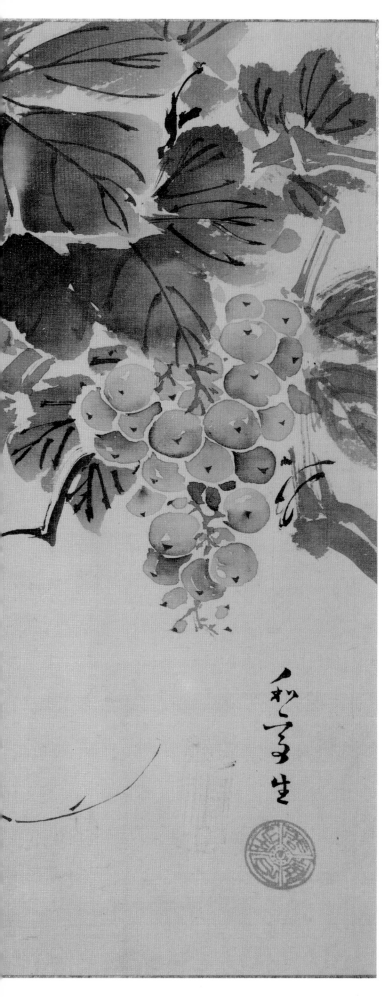

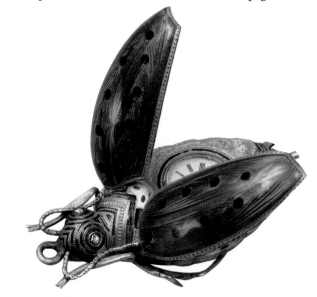

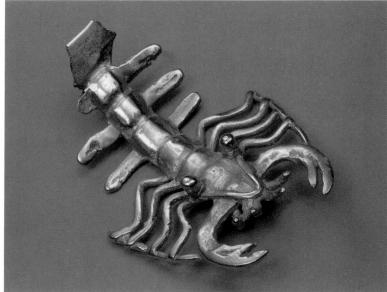

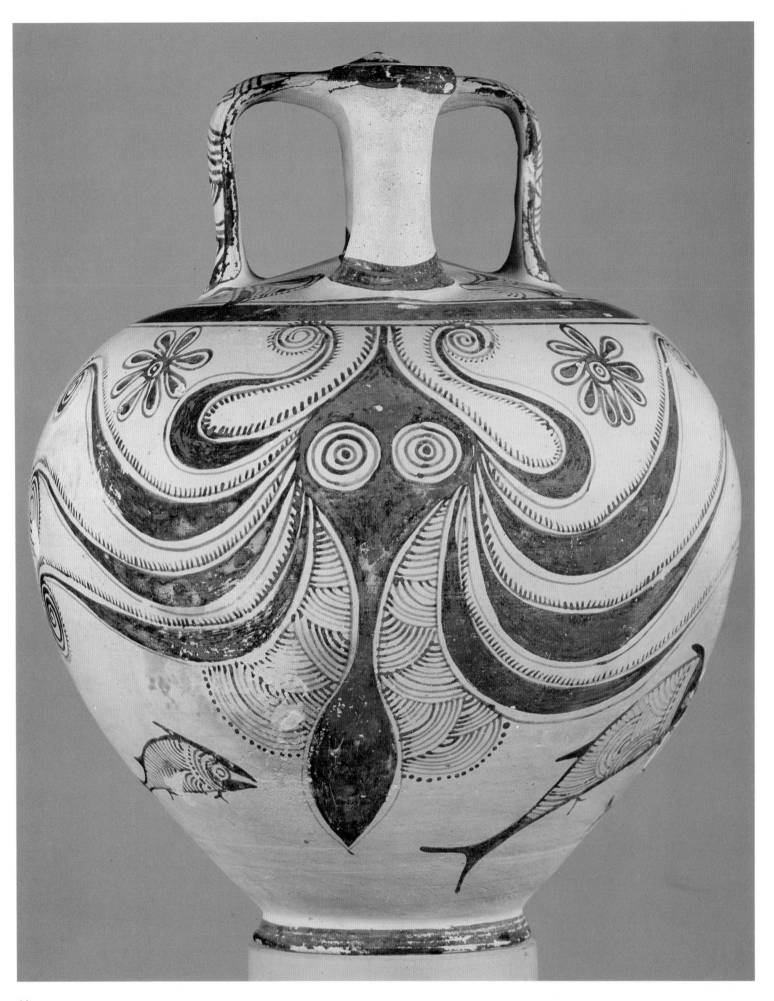

Octopus Stirrup Jar. The octopus lives in the murky depths of the ocean, usually tucking its flaccid, baglike body into a rocky crevice and snagging food with its sinuous tentacles. Its appearance alone has earned it an evil reputation, for the octopus is actually a rather timid creature that is truly dangerous only to the marine life it preys upon. A beautifully stylized octopus decorates one side of the terra-cotta stirrup jar (opposite) from Mycenae, dating to the twelfth century B.C. The ancient Greeks were a seafaring people, and jars like this were probably used to store liquids, such as oil or wine, during their long voyages.

Ceremonial Coverlet. Of all the 25,000 or more joint-legged animals classified as crustaceans, lobsters are perhaps the best known and certainly the most enjoyed. Caught by the millions each year, they are marketed as a culinary delicacy around the world. The spiny lobster painted on the nineteenth-century Japanese Yogi cotton coverlet below is a species found in tropical waters. Yogi coverlets are a type of bedding in kimono form used on special occasions. This one celebrates the new year; the lobster, curved like the bent-over figure of an old man, and the mandarin oranges signify a wish for long life. The round figure at the top is a family crest.

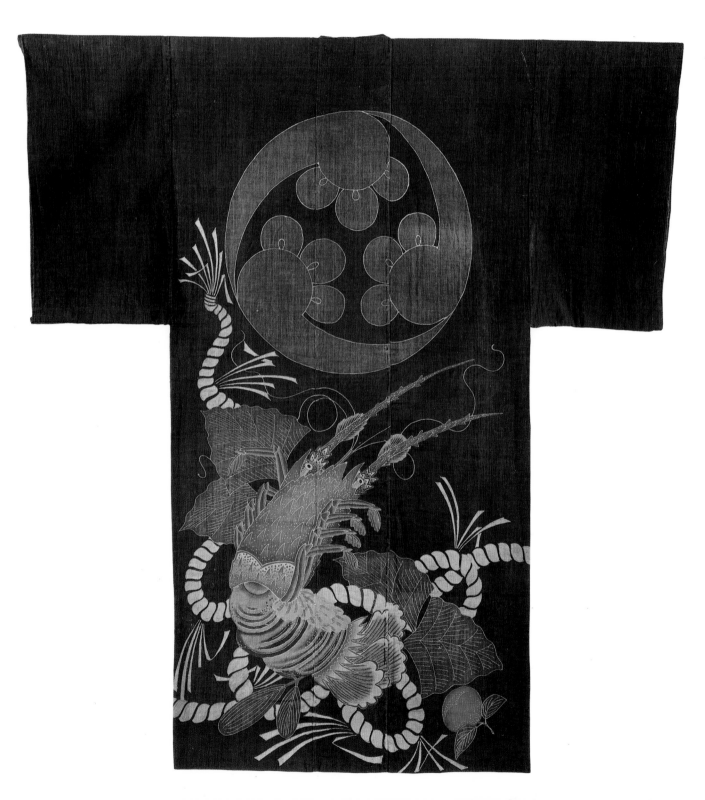

Underwater Marine Life. More than seven-tenths of the planet we live on is covered by water. Beneath the surface of its oceans, seas, lakes, ponds, rivers, and streams exists a world much older than ours, inhabited by many creatures that are the same now as they were millions of years ago, long before the first amphibian crawled up on dry land and breathed air. A glimpse of this vast underwater environment can be seen in this drawing by Christian Schuessele (American, 1824/6–79) and James M. Sommerville, made as a study for a chromolithograph published in 1860. The scene depicts in tremendous detail the colorful plant and animal life in a tropical American ocean. Among the corals, kelp, and sea anemones are sea snails, scallops, starfish, a seahorse, and several other species of fish.

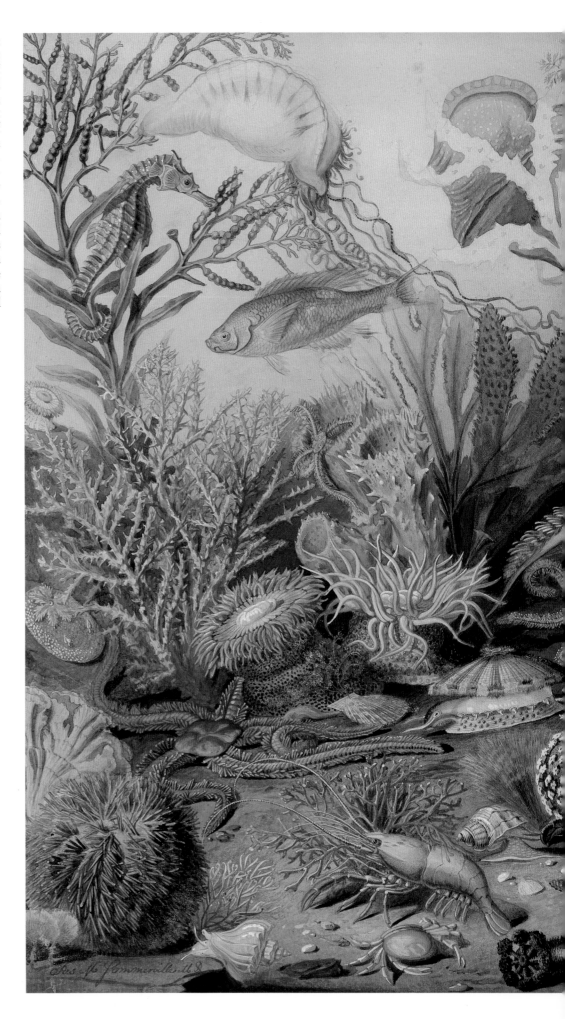

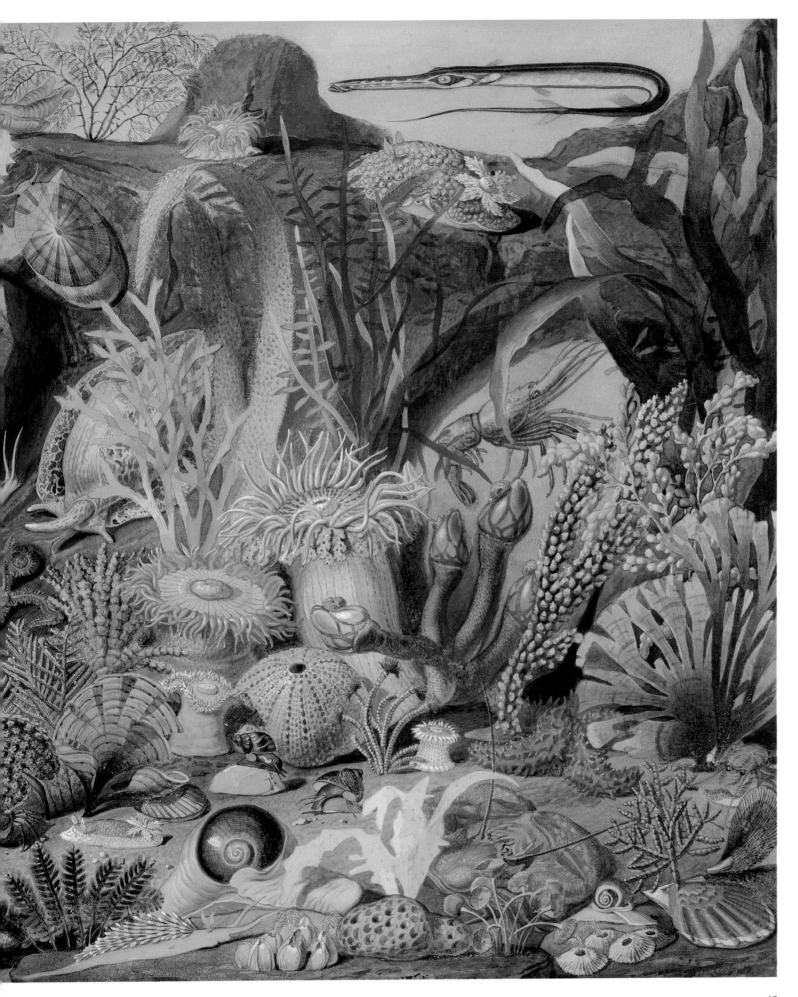

Campanian Fish Plate. Although fish vary considerably in size and shape to meet the needs of a particular habitat, in general they are sleek animals, contoured to offer the least resistance to an environment eight times denser than air. The most colorful species are found in the tropics, especially in the waters around coral reefs, but even those found in temperate seas present a dazzling array of forms and patterns, and they have captured the imagination of artists throughout history. The fish plate below was made in the late fourth century B.C. by a Greek artist working in Italy, yet it is very contemporary in feeling. The larger fish, possibly types of wrasse or bream, are too stylized for positive identification, but the lutelike shape of the torpedo—a kind of ray—is easily recognizable. The torpedo is capable of delivering a strong electric charge when capturing prey or defending itself against other predators.

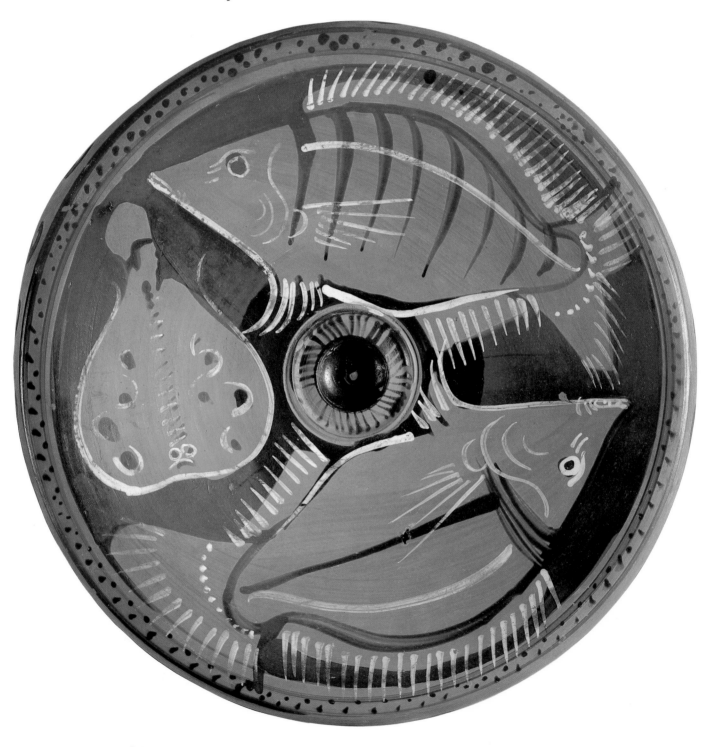

Gruel Bowl. Fish are the oldest of all the world's back-boned animals; although the branches of their family tree do not extend above the water's surface, its roots go down about 450 million years. More than 20 thousand species have been described, and some kind of fish can be found almost anywhere there is water. Fish have always been a major food source for humans. About seventy million tons are taken from the water annually, and the demand increases every year. The porcelain bowl below, perhaps designed to hold a steaming fish broth, was made in France in 1745. The bowl itself is shaped like a carp, but the scene on its side, curiously, is that of a boating couple—who do not appear to be fishing—framed by a bird and flowers.

The Pleasure of the Fishes. "Ah, the fish are happy," observed Chuang-tzu. His companion gazed from the same bridge down at the same fish and wondered, "You are not the fish. How can you know that they are happy?" Chuang-tzu replied, "You are not I. How can you know what I know?" This legendary encounter spurred centuries of speculation on the nature of knowledge as well as the common wisdom that of all living creatures fish are most in harmony with their surroundings. Fish appear in countless forms in Chinese art as emblems of wealth and abundance, of marital felicity, and as symbols of regeneration. Signifying freedom from all restraints, fish suggest the condition of the enlightened man to Buddhists. The carp in particular, seen here with its scaly armor, symbolizes martial attributes and also represents perseverance since it swims upstream through rough rapids.

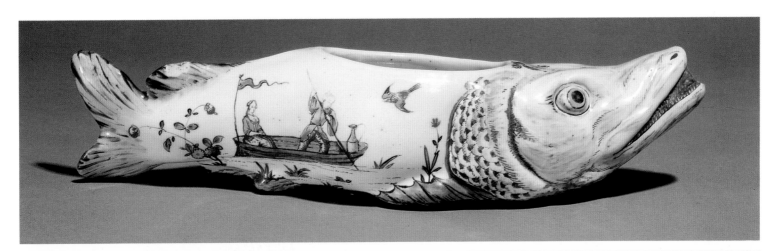

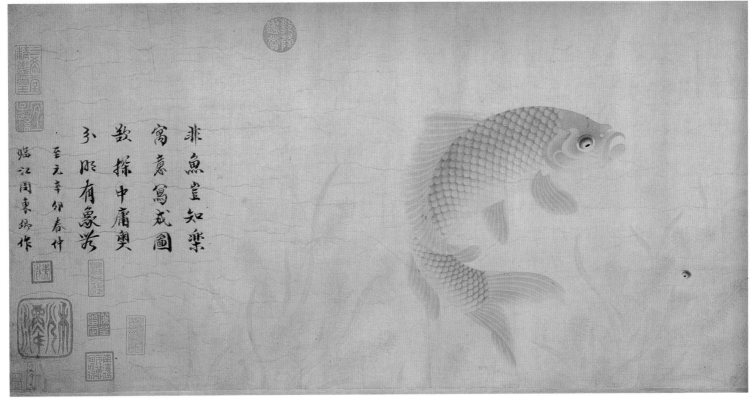

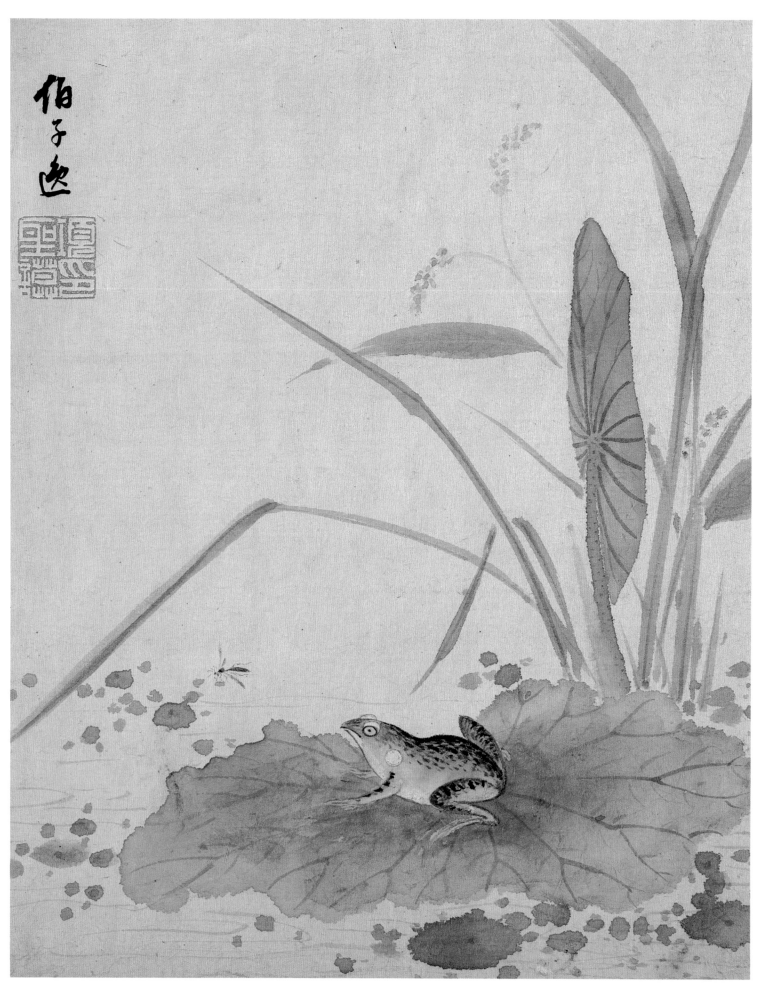

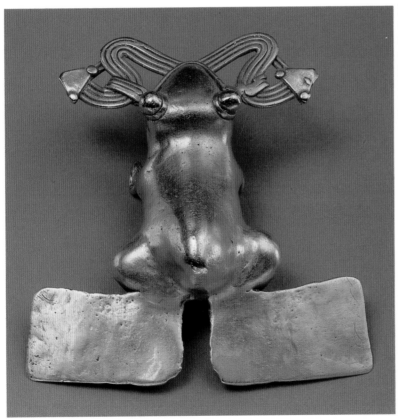

Frog Pendant. In the American tropics, there are a number of small, jewel-like species of frogs that, despite their decorative appearance, are highly venomous. The cast-gold pendant (left) is from Panama and probably represents one of them. Like the crayfish pendant on page 65, the frog was made sometime between the eleventh and sixteenth centuries, and while it may have had a ritualistic purpose—portraying a creature potentially harmful to humans—its true significance is not known.

Frog Automaton. Although the spring peeper is known for its beautiful evening serenade, the sound made by most frogs is limited to a croak or a grunt, and this nineteenth-century Swiss automaton is no exception. Beneath its enamel and gold surface, which is set with rubies and pearls, is a clockwork mechanism that not only produces croaks but also moves its legs while propelling the frog on tiny wheels.

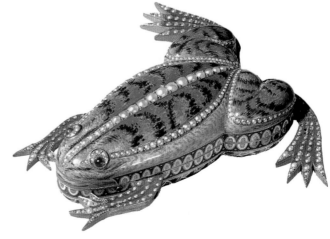

Frog on a Lotus Leaf. "Oh, to be a frog, my lads, and live aloof from care," wrote Theocritus in the late third century B.C. That worthy Greek may have been a fine poet, but no frog could be free of care when its position on the food chain renders it vulnerable to any passing pike, snake, or heron. "On your toes" would be a better motto, and the frog opposite, poised for a quick departure at the first sign of danger, is certainly on its. An ink and color painting on paper, this is one of eight leaves in an album of birds and flowers by the Chinese artist Hsiang Sheng-mo (1597–1658). The lotus is a symbol of purity in China because, although it rises from the muck of the pond, its blossom is pure and unsullied. It thus offers hope to people mired in the complications of a mundane world.

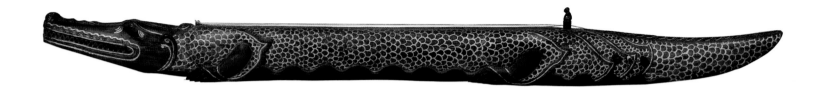

Crocodile Zither. A living relic of the age of reptiles one hundred million years ago, the fearsome crocodile is still found in tropical waters in many parts of the world. The crocodile-shaped instrument below, called a *mi gyaun*, was made in southern Burma from a single piece of hollowed teak. It has three strings, and the details of the reptile's body are painted in gold. A *mi gyaun* was played by Burmese musicians when they visited the Chinese imperial court during the ninth-century T'ang dynasty.

Crocodiles. The American alligator, cousin to the crocodile, is another species whose ancestry dates to the time when reptiles dominated the earth; it is now found only in the southern United States. The watercolor below by John Singer Sargent (American, 1856–1925) shows alligators (*not* crocodiles, in spite of the title of the painting) in a typical setting as they bask on a mudbank. Only two of the animals are rendered in detail, but the artist has captured the power and grace of all seven.

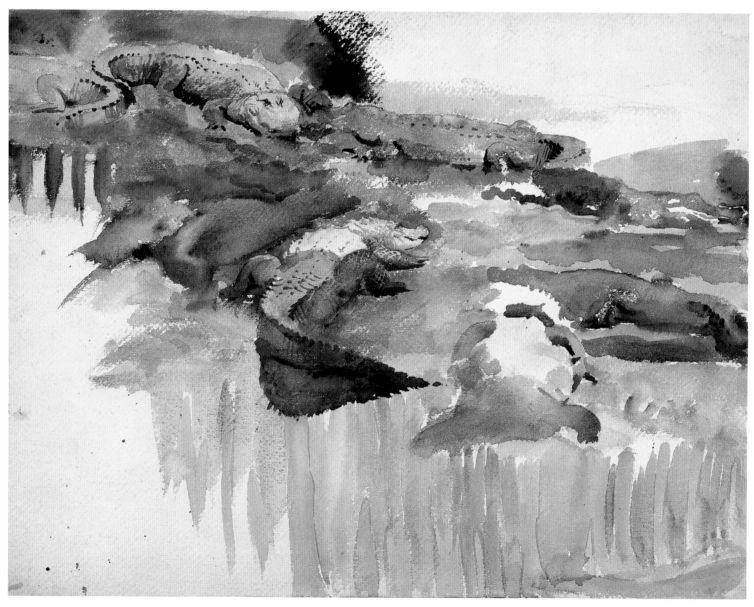

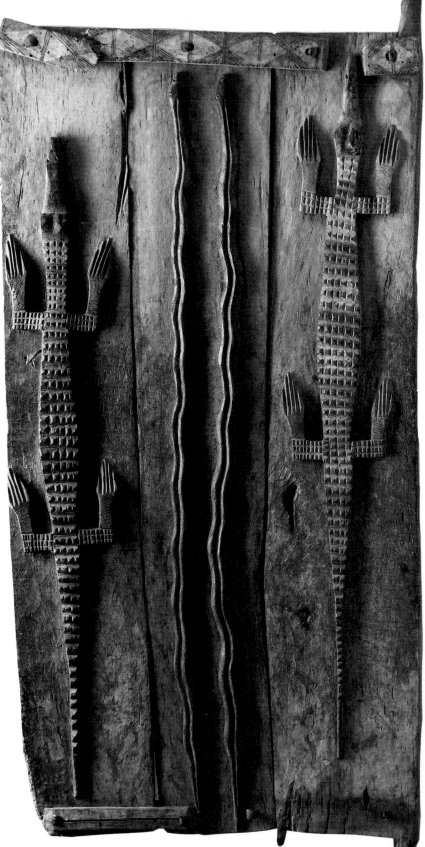

Crocodile Door. Crocodiles are still fairly common along most African rivers. Both feared and respected, they often figure in African art, as on these carved wooden doors made by the Bamana or Bozo people of Mali. In Africa, crocodiles and snakes are often associated with water spirits and may appear in art as messengers to the supernatural world.

Butter Box. Carrying their own defensive armor on their backs, tortoises have no great need to hurry. Their metabolic rate is so low that they can go for months without eating when food is scarce, and species native to temperate regions regularly hibernate in winter. The tortoise figure shown below is a Meissen butter box made of hard-paste porcelain in Germany around 1725. The carapace forms the cover.

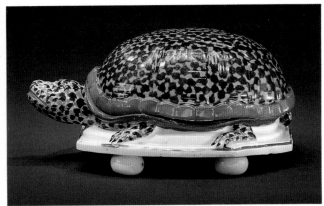

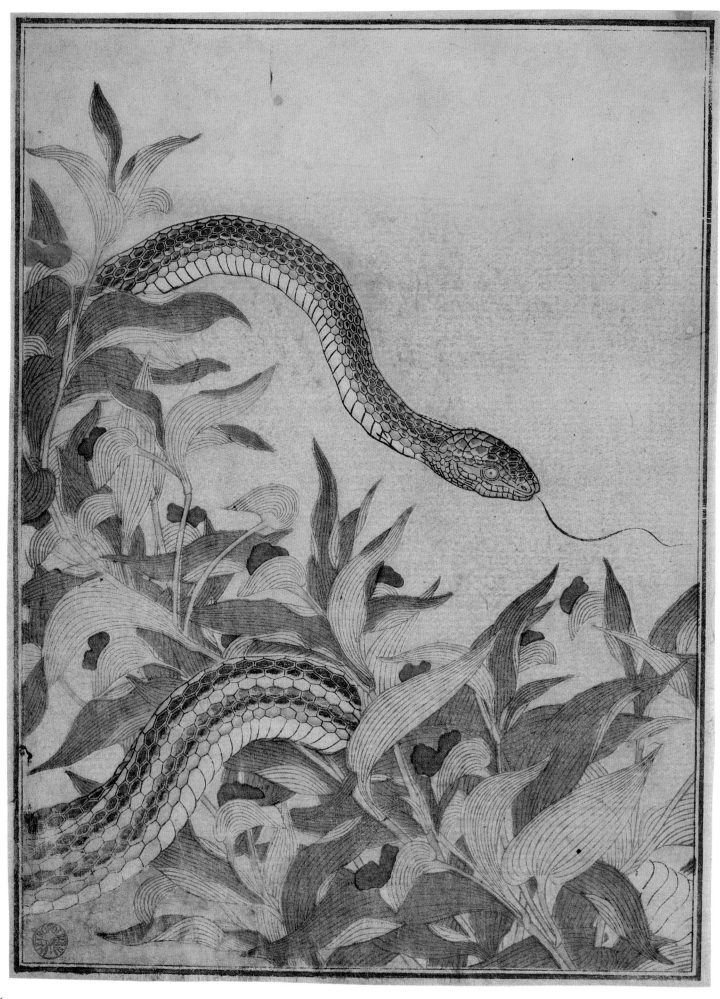

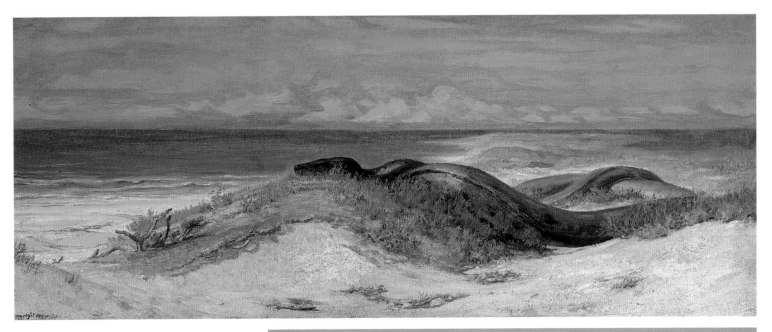

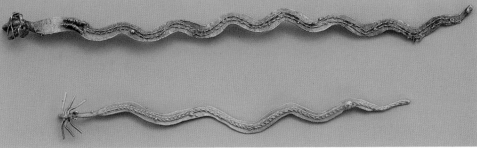

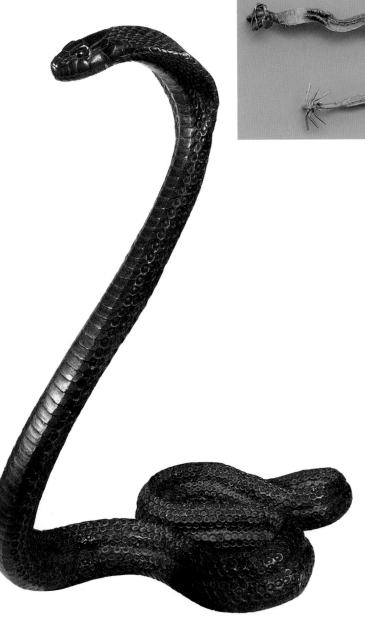

Rat Snake. Of all living creatures, snakes are easily the most feared and least understood. Found on all the earth's major land masses, snakes have nevertheless been shrouded with an air of mystery because of their secretive ways, their power to envenom, and their unique form of locomotion. The grace and beauty of the reptile in its natural environment, however, are clearly depicted in the woodblock print (opposite) of a rat snake winding its way through a dayflower plant. Designed by the Japanese artist Kitagawa Utamaro (1753–1806), the print is one of fifteen that appear in *Ehon mushi erabi* (*Picture Book of Selected Insects*), a book of garden images published in 1788.

Lair of the Sea Serpent. Tales of giant sea serpents have colored the annals of seafaring lore for centuries. The American artist Elihu Vedder (1836–1923) created such a monster in the painting reproduced above by envisioning a large anaconda on a beach. Although the anaconda is basically a water snake, it lives in the warm jungle rivers of South America, not along the seashore.

Gold Snakes. The two gold serpents shown above are known as *tunjos*, animal-shaped objects made by the Muisca people of central Colombia from perhaps the tenth to the sixteenth century. Their purpose was votive, and it is likely that they had some religious or mythological significance.

Cobra. A snake mystique figures in the art and culture of many lands. To the ancient Egyptians, the cobra was Uraeus, the emblem of judgment and death. The bronze and gilt cobra at left was made in the twentieth century by the French designer Jean Dunand (1877–1942), and its very shape is frightening even to modern sensibilities.

Aquatic Birds at a Pool. The bird life of India is rich and varied; more than one thousand species have been recorded within its borders. In this turn-of-the-eighteenth-century leaf from a Mughal Indian album in the Museum's collection, some of the water birds found there are shown assembled at a marshy pond. Prominent among them is a greater flamingo (the large pink and white bird) and a purple swamp hen, a kind of gallinule. The waterfowl include a flying mallard drake, a swimming tree duck, and a ruddy shelduck and a Garganey teal spreading their wings at the lower right. A bittern has just successfully speared a wormlike creature for its dinner, while three finches take wing in the center of the painting and a pair of larks (or pipits) perch on a stump in the foreground. Although most of the birds are so clearly rendered that the exact species may be recognized, the finches and larks are too vaguely defined for any positive identification.

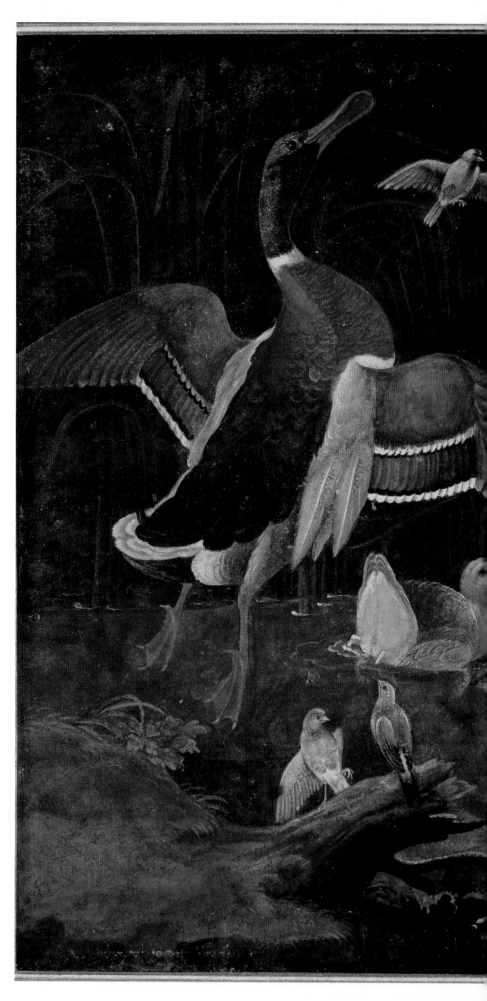

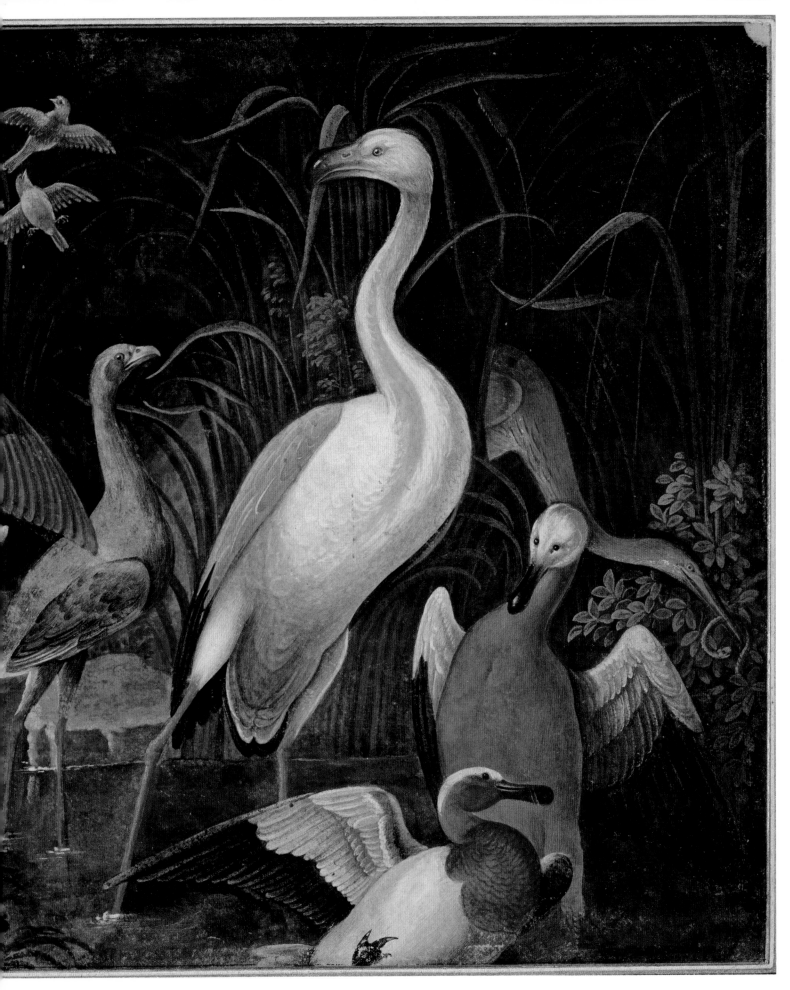

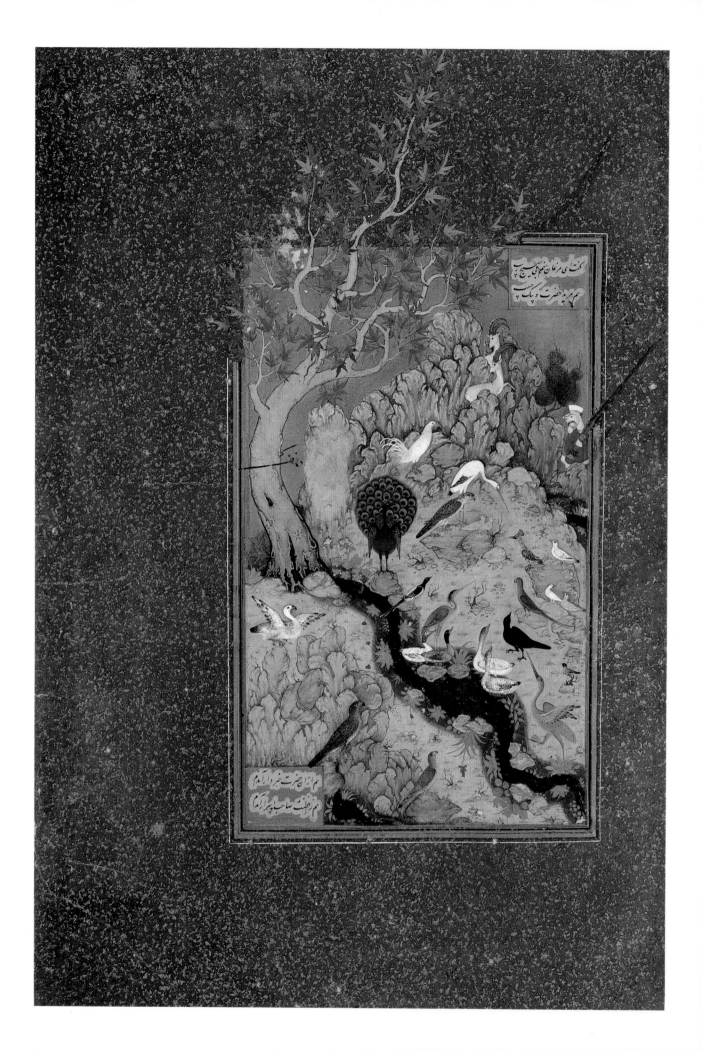

The Concourse of the Birds. A colorful array of hawks, herons, a peacock, a stork, and many other birds gathered together by a woodland stream is the subject of the scene (opposite) painted by the Iranian artist Habib Allah about 1600. It was executed on paper with colors, gold, and silver as the frontispiece for an edition of a twelfth-century poem by Farid-al-din'Attar called *Mantiq at-Tayr* (*The Language of Birds*). In the poem a hoopoe (the crested bird at right center) leads the others on a pilgrimage in search of a spiritual leader.

Japanese Crane. In this leaf from an album of flower and bird paintings by the Japanese artist Katei (1830–1901), an elegant crane stands precariously fluttering its wings in a fast-moving stream beneath a peach tree. These birds once ranged throughout much of eastern Asia during their long seasonal migrations, but they are now very rare, as precarious in nature as the bird appears to be in this painting. Known variously as the Manchurian crane, Chinese crane, Japanese crane, and the sacred crane, this bird has been regarded as a symbol of happiness and long life, and as such it is regularly represented in the art and folklore of the regions where it once lived. Although this painting was made by a Japanese artist during the late nineteenth century, it is stylistically reminiscent of the realist tradition of Chinese academic painting that dates back to the Sung dynasty.

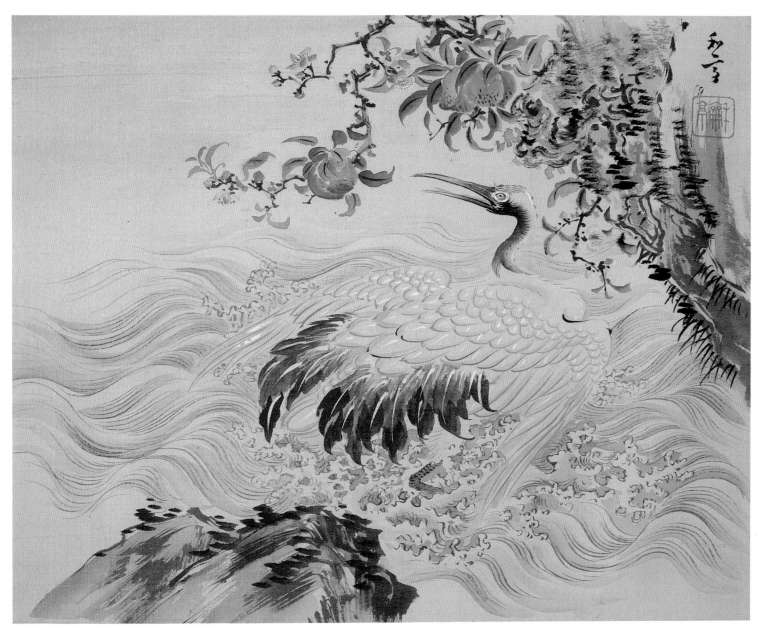

Peach Tree, Peonies, and Cranes. Although these birds are the same species as that on the previous page, they would probably be called Chinese rather than Japanese cranes, since the artist, Shen Ch'uan (1682–1758) was Chinese. The painting, a hanging scroll, can be dated to 1731–33, during the time when Shen Ch'uan, also known as Nanp'in, came to Nagasaki and brought to Japan the realistic style of Chinese academic painting. In spite of the difference in nationality and date, these two images of cranes (and their accompanying peaches) are remarkably similar. While the peach tree symbolizes immortality and springtime and is the emblem of marriage, peonies are held in high esteem as symbols of love, affection, and feminine beauty. Cranes signify longevity and are thought to convey the souls of the departed to the Buddhist Western Paradise.

Woodcock Tureens. Handsome as well as useful, the tin-glazed earthenware tureens illustrated on the opposite page were made in Germany in the mid-eighteenth century. Although quite accurate in detail, the tilted head and upturned bill are not a typical woodcock stance, but the arrangement does provide suitable handles for the tureen covers. Unlike most sandpipers, woodcocks live in dense woodlands far from the shore. Their special adaptations for forest life include mottled brown plumage for camouflage, large eyes for better vision in dim light, and a long bill with a flexible tip, useful in probing for earthworms, the woodcock's favorite food.

Herons. Ghostlike against a loosely defined background that includes only a few reeds, the birds in this Japanese hanging scroll are nevertheless easily distinguished as egrets, the graceful denizens of marshes and swamps around the world. Dated 1769, the scroll is drawn in ink on paper in the style of Maruyama Okyo (Japanese, 1733–95), who studied realistic Chinese and Western paintings and, in combination with decorative elements of Japanese art, synthesized his own style. Egrets were a favored subject for Japanese artists, and, like cranes, are relatively rare. Once slaughtered by the thousands for their decorative plumes, egrets are now protected in most countries.

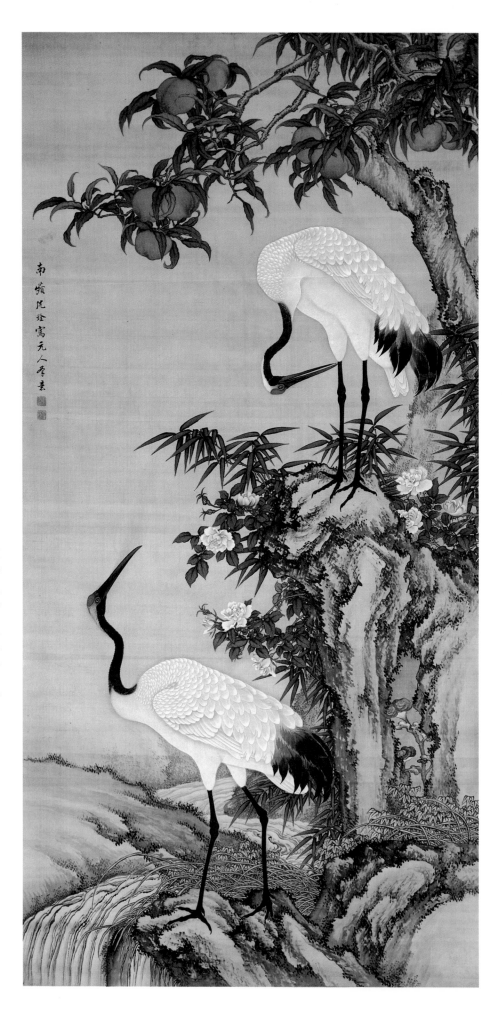

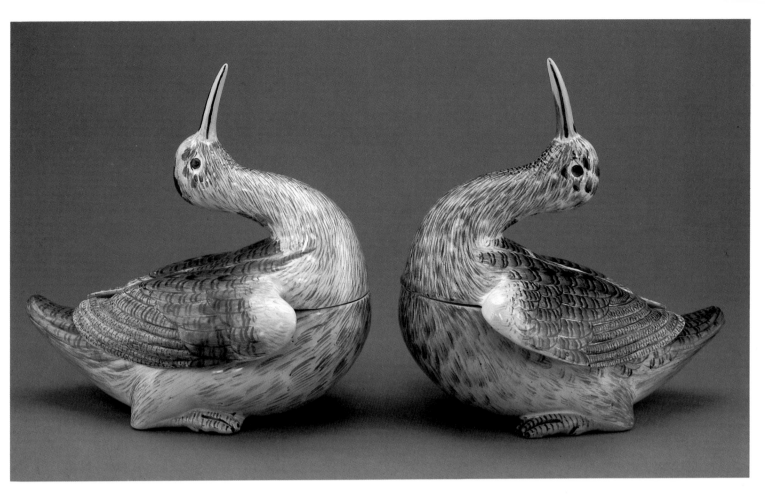

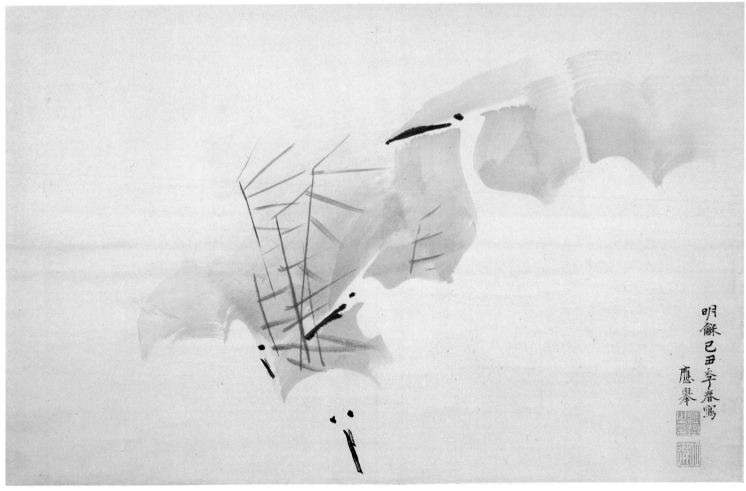

Angry Swan. Wild-eyed, its wings spread wide in a threatening gesture, a swan prepares to defend itself in this chalk-on-paper study by the painter Jean-Baptiste Oudry (French, 1686–1755). A specialist in the art of animal representation, Oudry was the official painter of the royal hunt for Louis XV and produced portraits of the king's favorite dogs as well as spectacular stag hunts, many of which were woven into tapestries. Oudry used this study of a swan in several paintings, frequently with the swan chased by dogs. Although swans are formidable in appearance and capable of delivering powerful blows with their wings, they are seldom really aggressive except when defending their young. Artists have often chosen swans as a subject because of their extraordinary beauty and grace; one species of swan is even named after the artist Thomas Bewick (see page 13), who described and illustrated it in his book *The History of British Birds*.

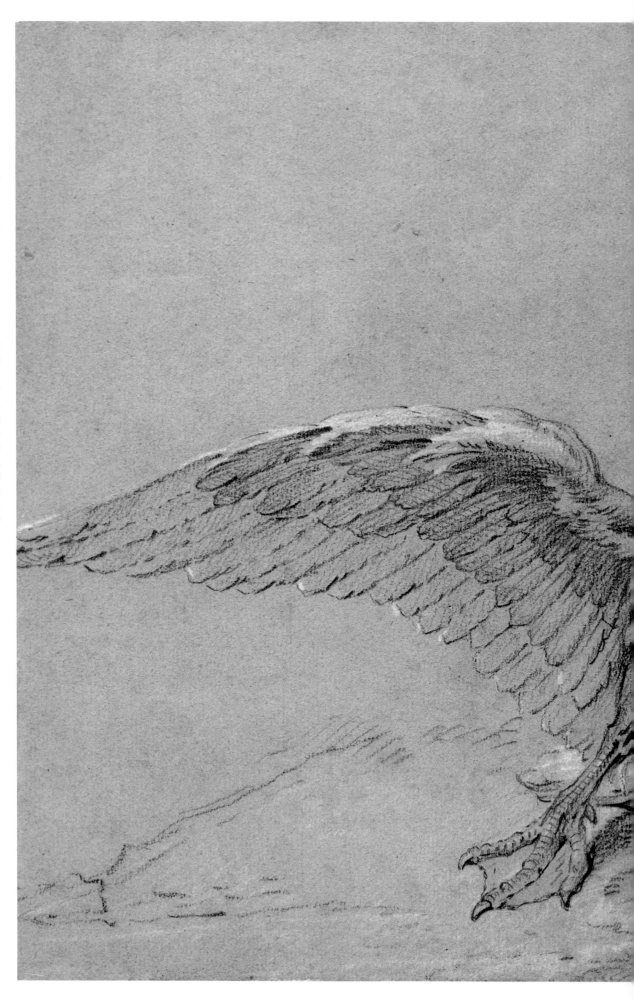

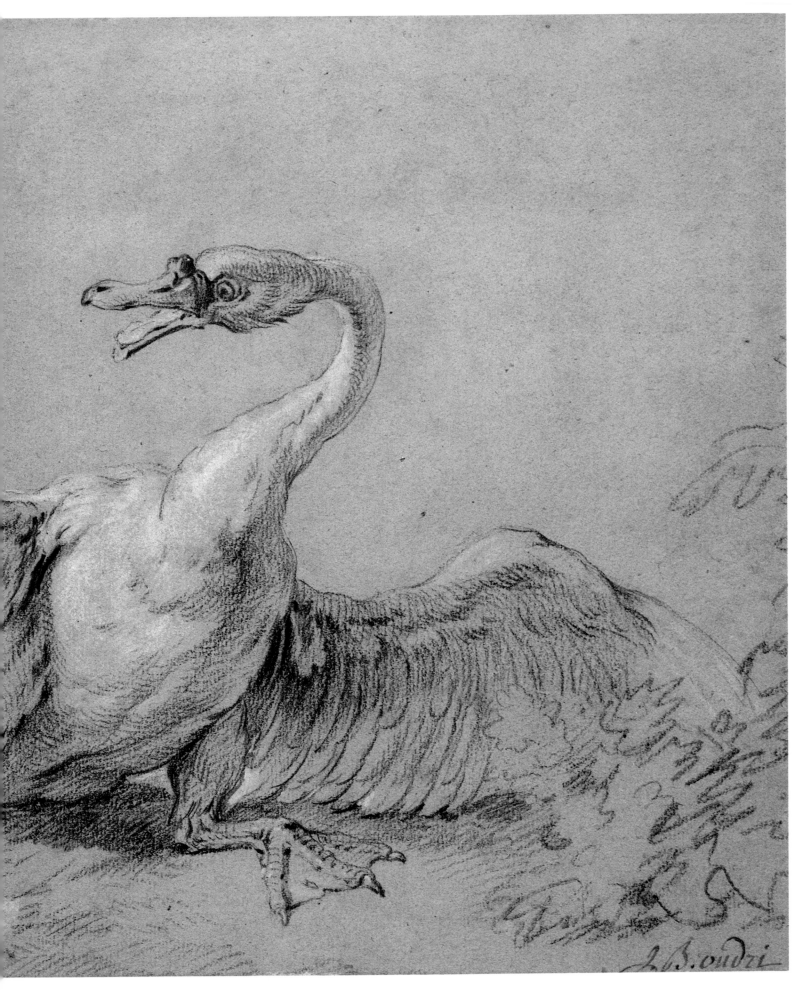

J. B. oudri

Three Swans. Although graceful in the water and powerful in flight, swans are clumsy creatures on land. Here, with the barest minimum of line and detail, John Singer Sargent (American, 1856–1925) has captured their awkward stance, with wings slightly dropped and neck drawn way back to counterbalance the forward distribution of weight. Native to Europe and Asia, mute swans were originally brought to the United States to grace the ponds of parks and large estates; the species is now well established along the eastern seaboard. Contrary to the name, mute swans can hiss, snort, and even make a whistling sound. Sargent, who was born in Italy to American parents, studied in Florence and Paris before settling in London, where he became best known for his portraits of English society. He also painted impressionistic landscapes and sketched out of doors, where he no doubt found his models for this pencil sketch.

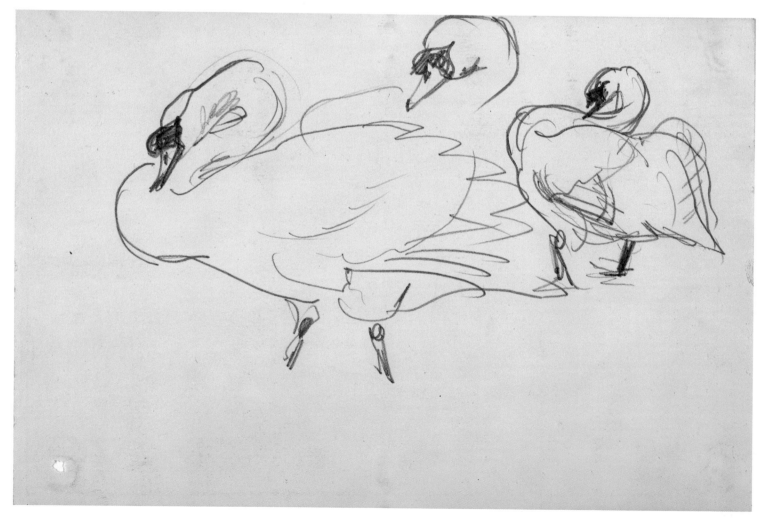

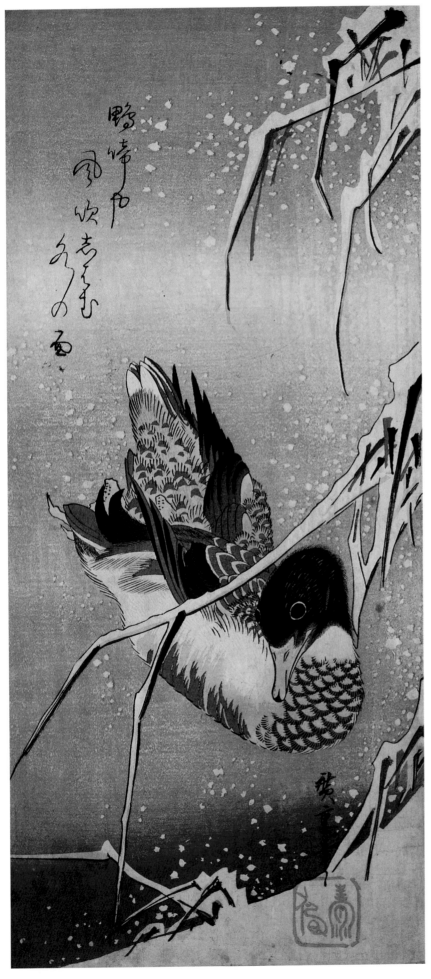

Wild Ducks in the Snow. The setting is a sylvan pond during what might well be the first snowfall of winter. Snowflakes are falling and the branches of the tree and the ground are already white, but the pond is not yet frozen and two ducks are afloat near the water's edge. One bird is only partially visible as it "tips up" in typical mallard fashion to feed from the bottom of the pond. This charming woodblock print was designed by the Japanese artist Andō Hiroshige (1797–1858). It is one of a series of prints he made featuring birds and flowers.

Waterfowl Vases. The two ceramic figures of water birds below were made in the sixth century B.C. The swan is from Corinth, while the duck, probably a pochard, is from eastern Greece. The pose of the two birds is similar, but the swan has been treated in a simple fashion that emphasizes its graceful shape. The chunky, bright-eyed little duck bears a pattern that outlines each feather, and its short legs have been positioned further forward than normal to provide a stable base for the vase.

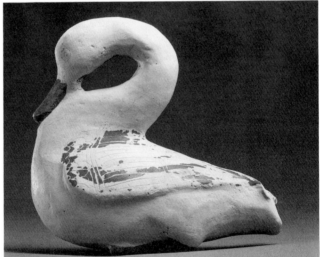

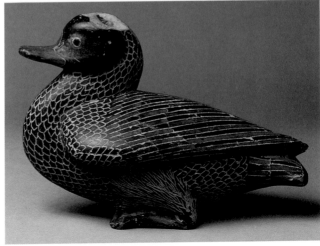

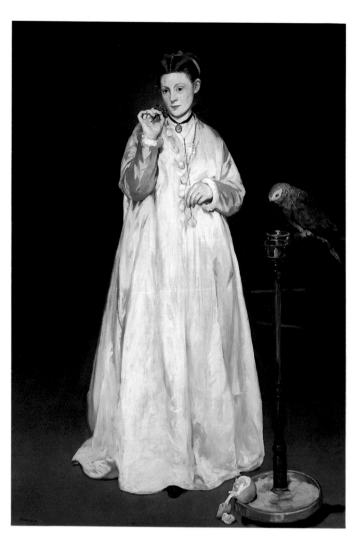

Woman with a Parrot. When this beautiful portrait was first exhibited by Edouard Manet (French, 1832–83), Paris art critics gave it scant notice, but the artist's friend Emile Zola recognized it as a masterpiece. The bird on the perch is an African gray parrot, a species highly prized for its ability to mimic the human voice and, thus, a popular household pet. Art historians have speculated on the allegorical meaning of the painting, since the subject is one that appears in the work of Gustave Courbet and even earlier in a seventeenth-century Dutch painting by Frans van Mieris. Although it seems to be a simple portrait, Manet may have intended to imply a close relationship between the woman and her parrot, who is a kind of confidant, an intimate companion aware of the secrets of her personal life.

Bronze Parrot. The perched figure of a ring-necked parakeet (below) was made in India during the eighteenth century. The position of the bird's right foot indicates that it may once have held some item, perhaps food. The bird, though stylized in form, is depicted quite accurately for the most part, except that the artist has very generously provided it with an extra toe on each foot.

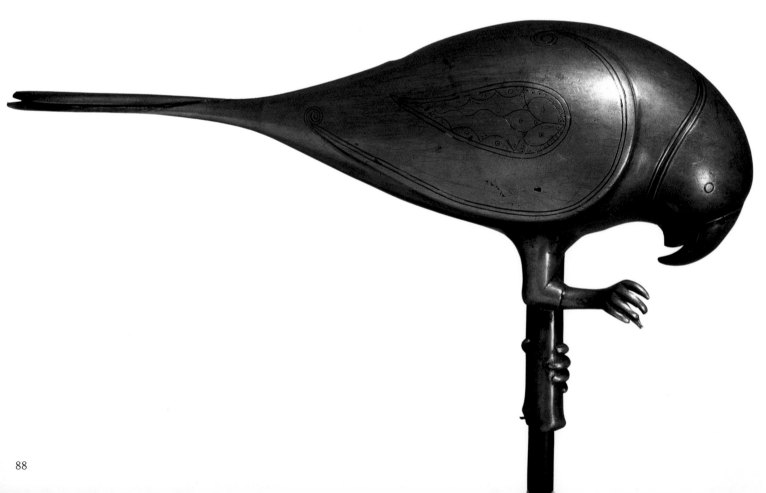

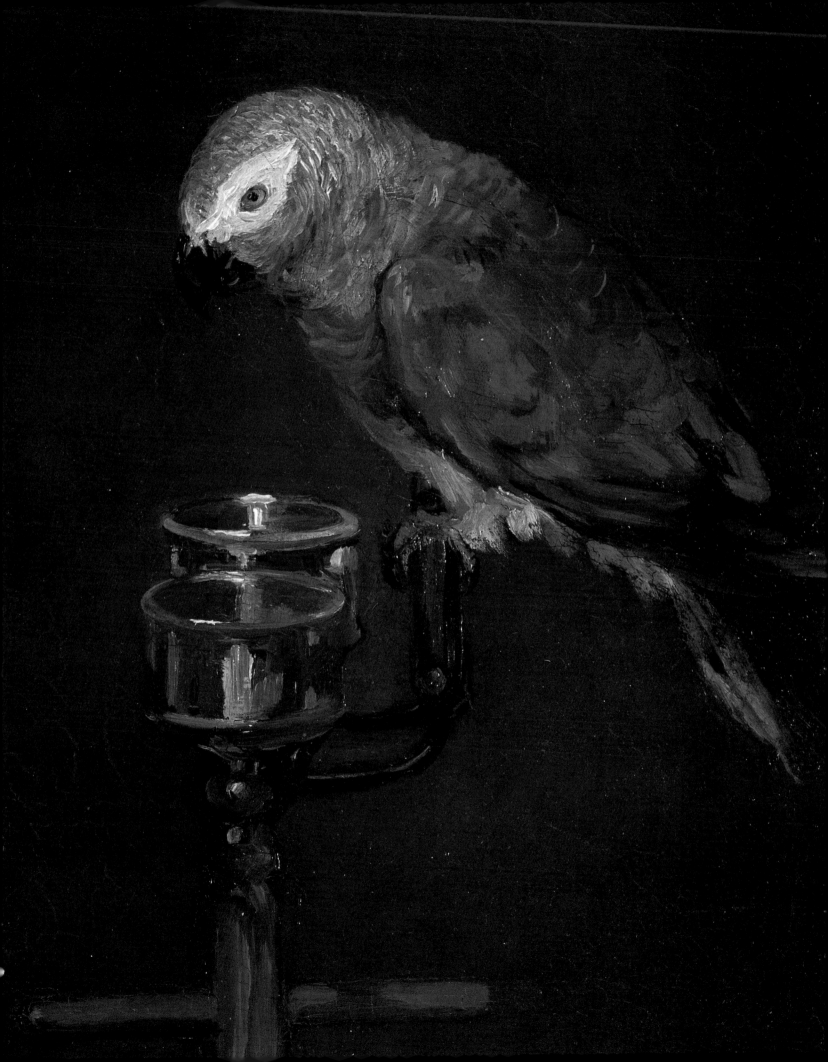

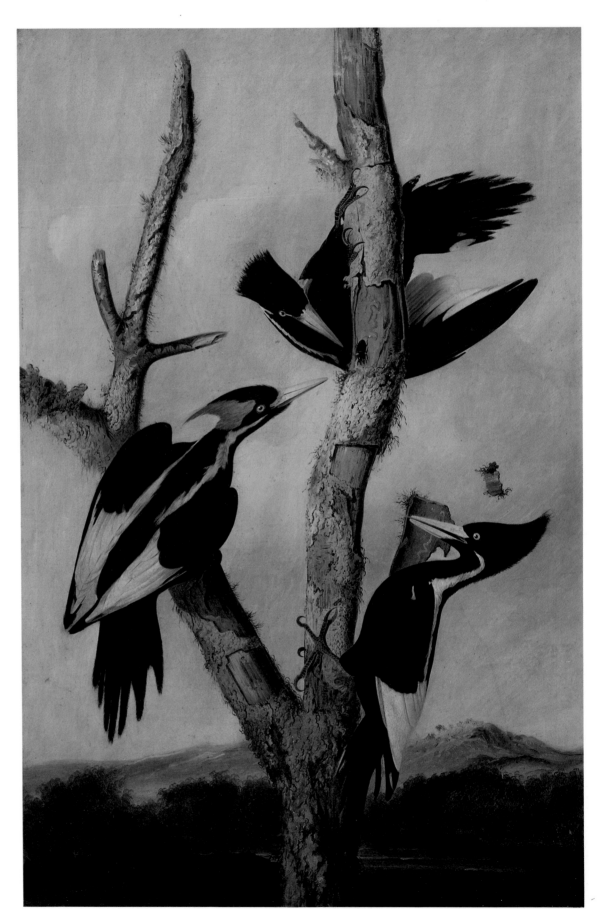

Ivory-billed Woodpeckers.
These are among the rarest of all North American birds. Destruction of their natural habitat, the swamps and woodlands of the southeastern United States, and the collection of specimens by enthusiasts brought them to the point of extinction by the beginning of the twentieth century, and it is very doubtful that any remain. These birds, like the extinct passenger pigeon and Carolina parakeet, were abundant, however, when John James Audubon (American, 1785–1851) published his monumental four-volume work, *The Birds of America*, which included 435 plates made from scenes such as the one illustrated here. Audubon commissioned the Scottish painter J. B. Kidd to copy this composition in oil.

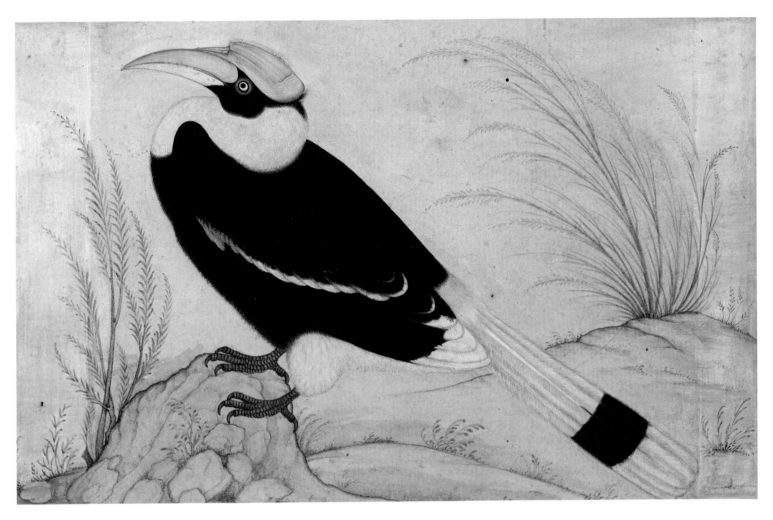

The Great Hornbill. A distant relative of kingfishers, this is one of the largest members of the hornbill family. The hornlike protuberance above the bill looks massive, but it is actually quite light in weight. The great hornbill is an Indian species, and this sheet is one of thirty-seven leaves in the album of human and animal portraits assembled in the seventeenth century for Shah Jahan. (See also pages 51 and 93.)

The Ostrich Hunt. Largest of all living birds, a full-grown male ostrich may stand nearly eight feet tall and weigh over 300 pounds. Although flightless, the bird has long, powerful legs that can carry it at speeds over thirty miles an hour. The ostriches in this print by Stefano della Bella (Italian, 1610–64) appear to be either females or young birds because of their generally uniform color; adult males have jet-black bodies with white wing tips and tails, feathers once highly prized by milliners. Formerly found as far north as Asia Minor, ostriches are now limited in their habitat to the grassy plains and deserts of Africa.

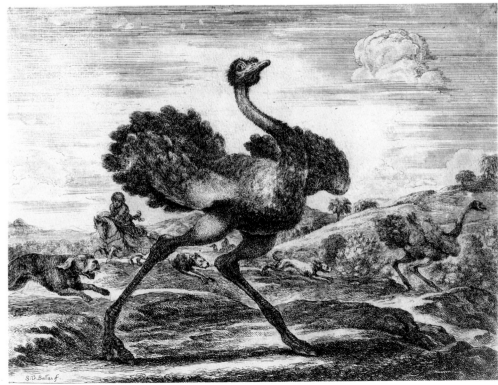

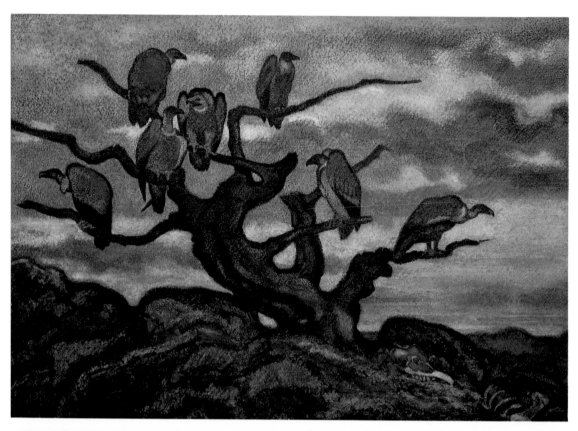

Vultures on a Tree. Generally reviled because of their macabre appearance and carrion-eating habits, vultures are nonetheless very important members of the natural cycle. Antoine-Louis Barye (French, 1796–1875) has effectively expressed the menace of these birds, which seem to await tragedy so that they can swoop down to investigate. Barye's own knowledge of animals has served him well here, for he has elected to depict the griffon vulture, a highly gregarious species that often roosts in groups.

Vulture Painting. The ancient Egyptians viewed the vulture, in certain contexts, as the representation of their goddess Nekhbet, patron deity of Upper Egypt and a protectress of the king. In this copy of a wall painting from the 18th-dynasty (about 1490 B.C.) Anubis chapel in Hatshepsut's temple at Deir el Bahri, the vulture goddess is seen holding the *shen* hieroglyph, which seems to signify eternity. The vulture is beautifully detailed in every feature and feather; the unnaturally vivid coloration was probably affected for decorative purposes.

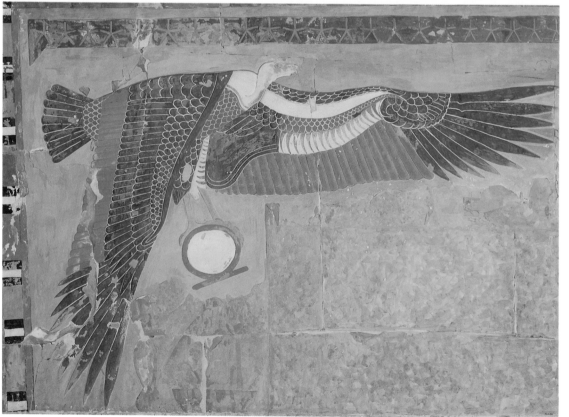

Two Vultures. Among the handsomest of Old World vultures are the Indian black vulture and the griffon vulture depicted here in precise detail with colors and gold, possibly by Mansur, the master court painter for Shah Jahan for the Emperor's album. (See also pages 51 and 91).

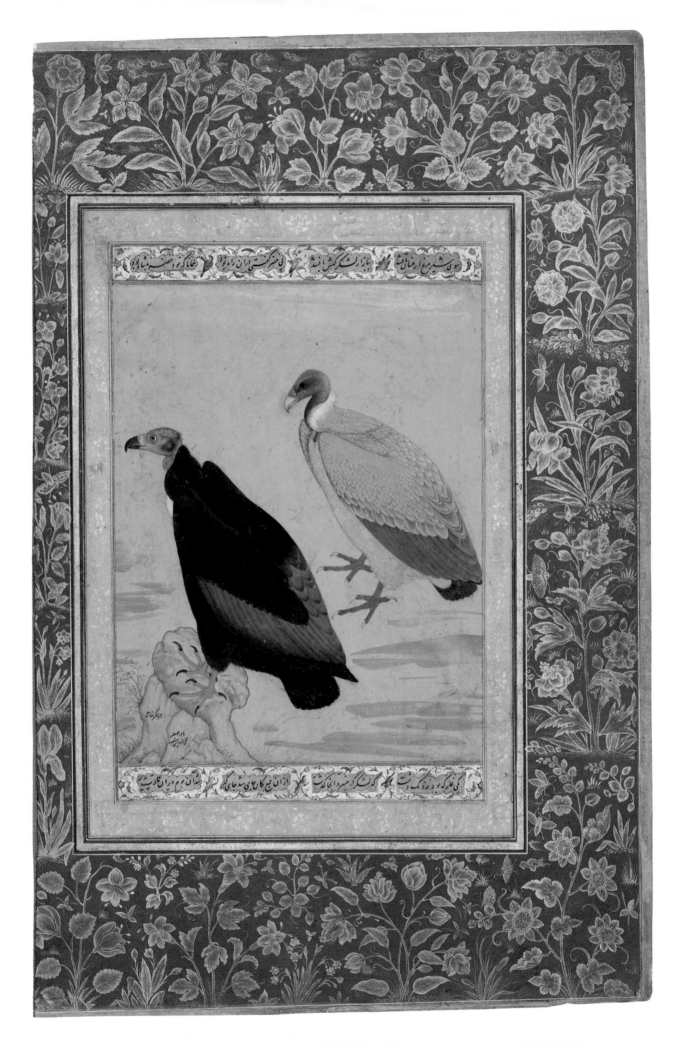

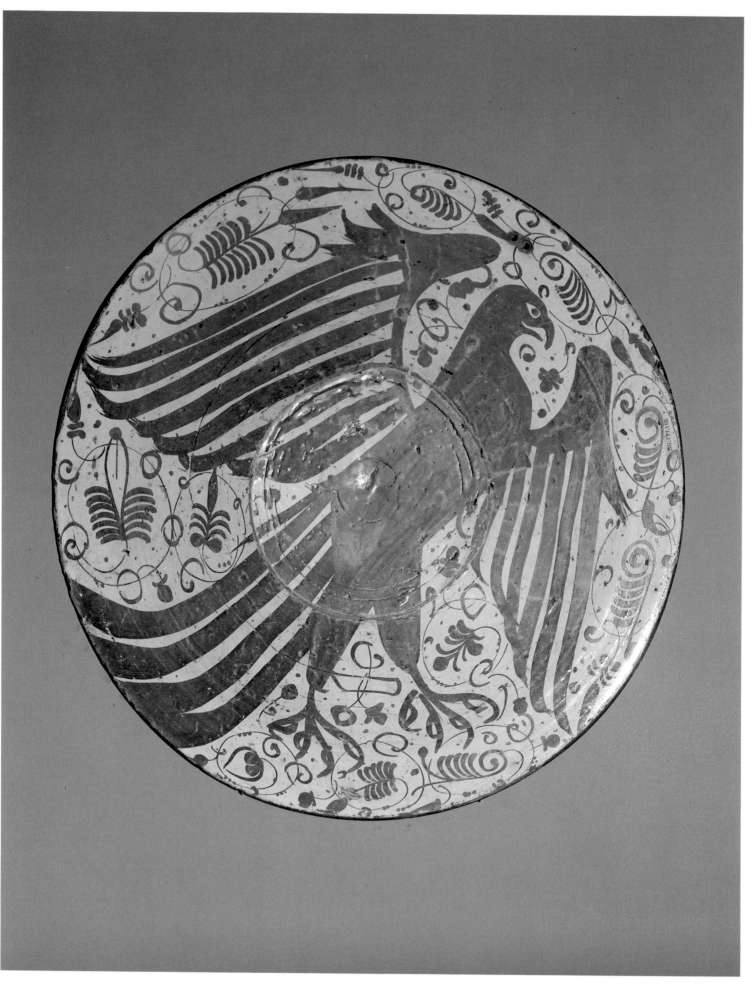

Eagle Dish. Bold hunters and superb fliers, birds of prey have held a special place in the cultures of many civilizations. Eagles especially, because of their impressive size and beauty, have often been used to symbolize royal power, from ancient Egypt to the Roman and Napoleonic empires, when they appeared on coins, standards, and other official objects. Eagles were also popular as design elements in pottery; the fifteenth-century Spanish plate (opposite) is a fine example of the famous lusterware produced in Valencia. Finished with a unique glazing process, the plate has the rich sheen of precious metal.

Eagle Lectern. In the bestiaries of the Middle Ages, the eagle was frequently depicted in relationship to the sun. Old eagles were thought to fly to the sun, then return to earth and plunge into a fountain three times to achieve rejuvenation, a belief possibly based on the fact that eagles, like other raptors, can achieve great height in flight. This behavior may be seen as a symbol of the rite of baptism, which may account in part for the presence of eagle images in medieval churches. The eagle was also the symbol for the apostle Saint John. This marble lectern has been identified as the one carved in Carrara marble by Giovanni Pisano in 1301 for the church of San Andrea in Pistoia, Italy.

Bird Mask. This striking mask was produced by a member of the Haida tribe in British Columbia during the nineteenth or early twentieth century. It probably represents an eagle—relatively common in Canada and Alaska, although their numbers are decreasing elsewhere in North America— and clearly has some symbolic significance relating to the animal's fearsome power.

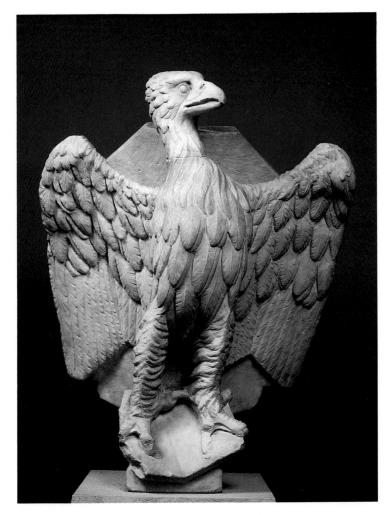

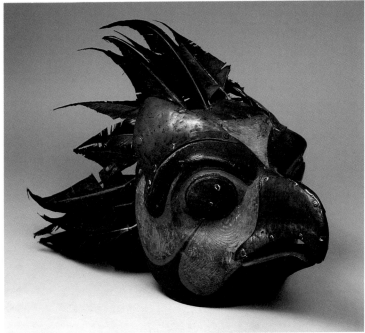

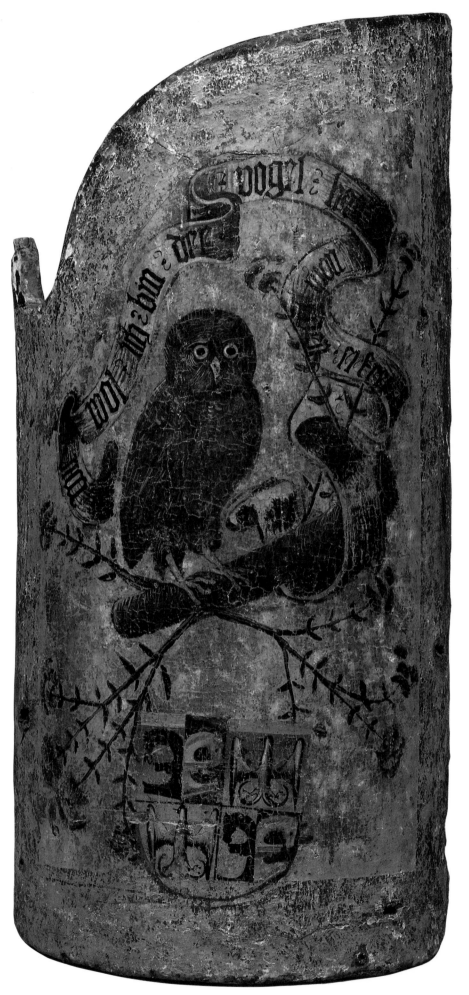

Jousting Targe. "Though I am hated by all birds, I nonetheless rather enjoy that" is a literal translation of the motto blazoned on this jousting shield of around 1500 along with the figure of an owl. While the standard was no doubt intended to provoke an adversary on the field of valor, it is also true that owls are feared by other birds, who recognize them as predators. When an owl's daytime roost is discovered, flocks of small birds "mob" the site, harassing the owl until it leaves the area. The shield, called a targe, is made of wood, pigskin, and burlap covered with gesso and paint. The notch on the left side was provided to support a lance in the couched position. The coat of arms is that of a Tyrolean family, Tänzi von Tratzberg, quartered with those of the barons of Rindscheit. It was probably used in tournaments held during the wedding celebration of Jakob von Tratzberg and Anna von Rindscheit in 1499.

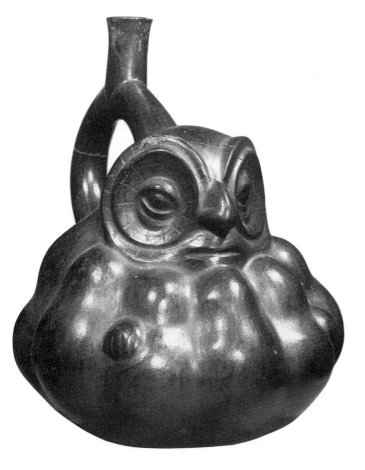

Stirrup-Spout Vessel. Owls are found almost everywhere on earth. One or more of the 130 species inhabit every land with the exception only of Antarctica and a few oceanic islands. The combination of their secretive, usually nocturnal ways and the human-like placement of their eyes has intrigued cultures throughout the world. Some civilizations have considered owls symbols of evil; others have believed them to be benevolent. The exact meaning of the owl on the ceramic container (left) is not known. The bird appears to be hatching from a squash and has distinctly human features, a combination not unusual in Precolumbian art. This vessel was fashioned by the Moche people of northern Peru, a culture that predated the Incas.

Two-handled Wine Cup. The ancient Greeks occasionally perceived owls as sinister creatures, while at other times they saw them as symbols of victory. The bird depicted on the fifth-century Attic two-handled wine cup below is the little owl *Athene noctua*, named for the goddess of wisdom, art, and warfare, who was sometimes portrayed with the owl, especially in fifth-century Athens.

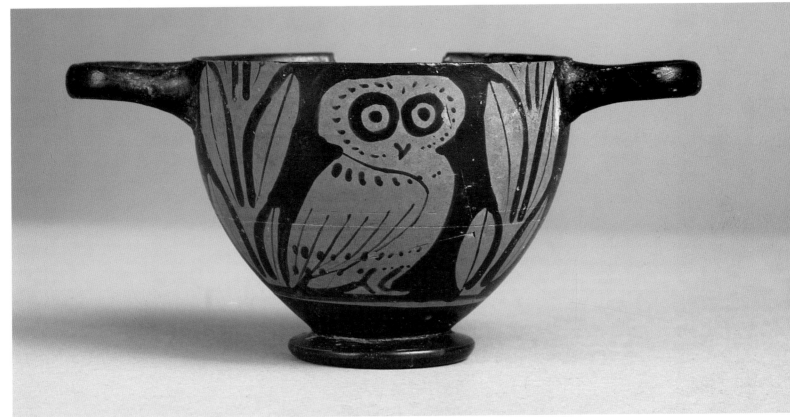

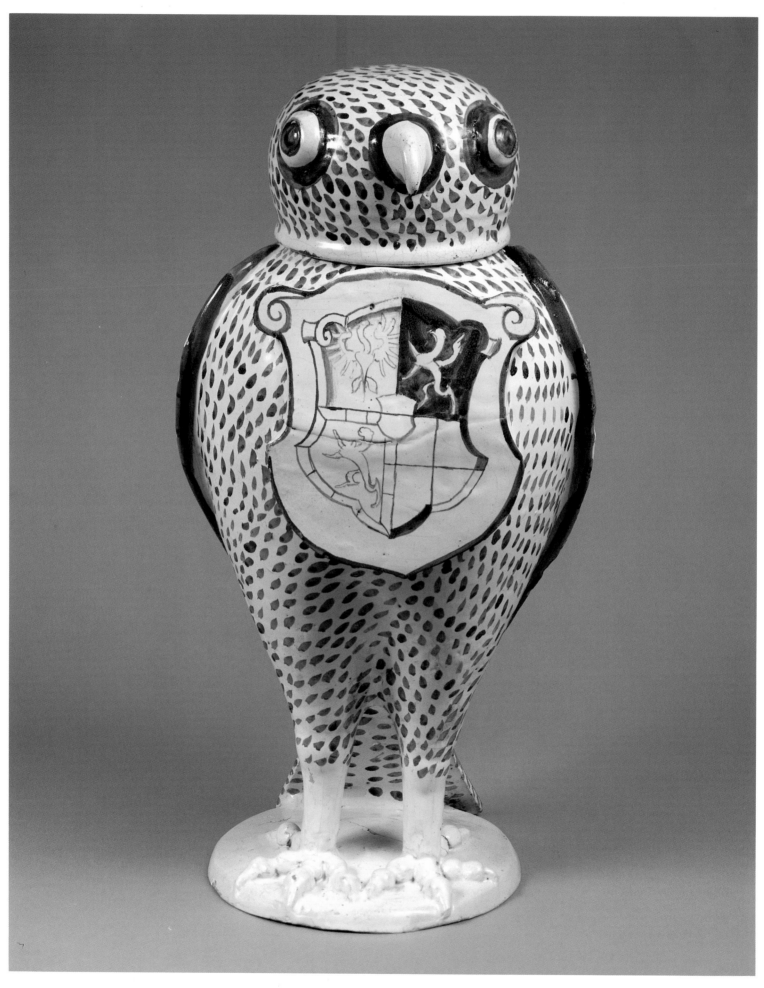

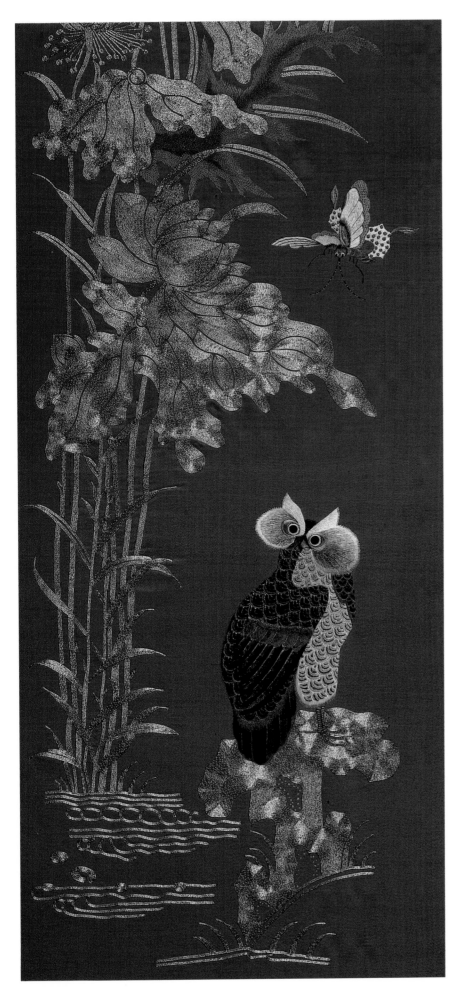

Owl Drinking Vessel. Owls vary in size, from those no larger than a sparrow to those approaching the dimensions of eagles. Many have tufts of feathers on their heads, like ears, while others lack them. But all owls have certain features in common—large eyes directed forward and facial disks of soft feathers that conceal huge ear openings—and all hunt, most of them at dusk or in darkness, so that keen vision and acute hearing are essential. These characteristics make owls recognizable even when their forms are radically stylized or simplified. The mid-sixteenth-century ceramic covered vessel from southern Germany illustrated on the opposite page bears the Hohenzollern coat of arms on its breast and has a removable head, but it is unmistakably an owl. The bird's body forms a flagon and the head can be used as a cup. Owl vessels are thought to have been prizes for events such as archery contests.

Owl Embroidery. The stylized bird in this detail from a nineteenth-century Chinese embroidery is easily recognized as an owl, considered to be an evil bird because the young are reputed to eat their mother, the ultimate unfilial behavior. The voice of the owl is heard with dread all over China as a harbinger of death in the neighborhood. Its distant hooting is thought to be the voice of a demoniac spirit.

Owl Finial. The small gold owl below was found in the Sinu region of Colombia in South America and was made sometime between the fifth and tenth centuries. The finial, which was probably attached to the staff of someone of high rank, resembles a modern-day caricature of an owl.

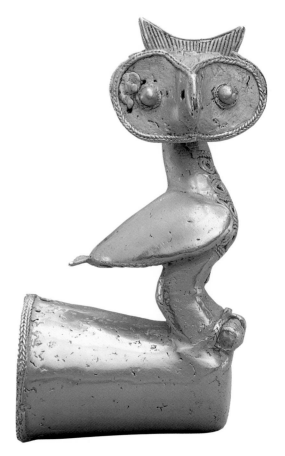

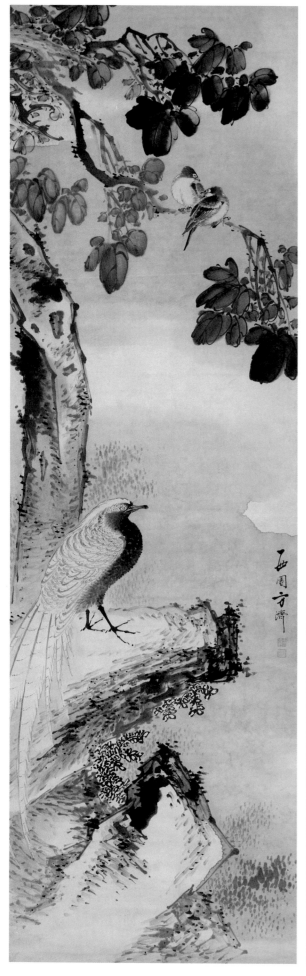

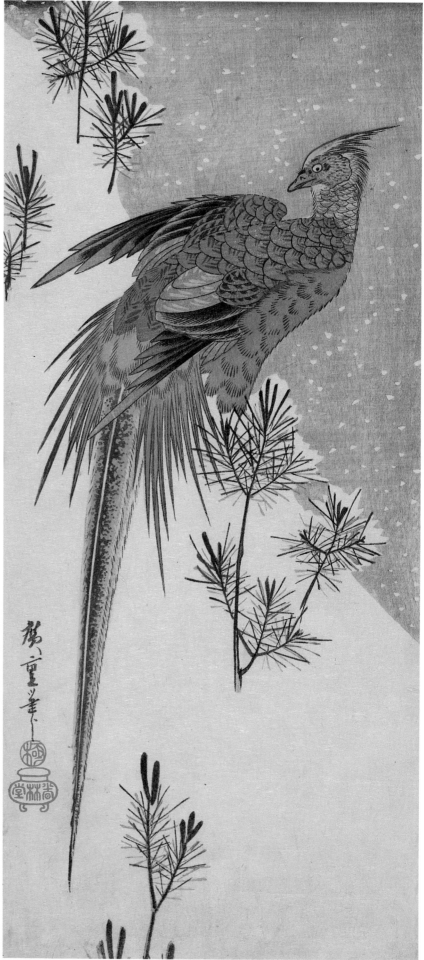

Pheasant Beneath Tree. Pheasants are the most spectacular of all the gallinaceous, or fowl-like, birds. There are about fifty species of "typical" pheasants (those in which the males have brightly colored plumage and long tails) and, with a single exception, all are native to Asia, so it is not surprising that pheasants have figured in Far Eastern art and literature through the centuries. The regal-looking pheasant shown at the left on the opposite page stands on a rocky crag beneath a peach tree in which are perched a pair of white-eyes, small fruit-eating birds common in the Far East. This hanging scroll was painted in ink on paper by the Chinese artist Fang Chi in the eighteenth century during the Ch'ing dynasty. It is interesting to note that Fang Chi went to Nagasaki in Japan in 1772, as many other Chinese artists had done, and that his realistic style of depicting nature was very influential in subsequent Japanese painting.

Pheasant Among Pines on a Snowy Declivity. To the right of the Chinese pheasant, opposite, another pheasant sits in the branches of an evergreen. This woodblock print is an excellent example of Hiroshige's exceptional powers of imagination and design as well as his knowledge of natural forms, for although the bird looks like a typical pheasant, it is not a true species but a hybrid created by the artist.

Ruffed Grouse. On the floor of a forest somewhere in North America, a ruffed grouse stretches its neck as it looks and listens for signs of approaching danger. This watercolor, painted by Gerald M. Thayer (American, 1883–1939), was used to illustrate the book *Concealing-Coloration in the Animal Kingdom*, written by the artist and his father in 1909. The cryptic pattern and muted colors of the grouse's plumage almost completely camouflage it.

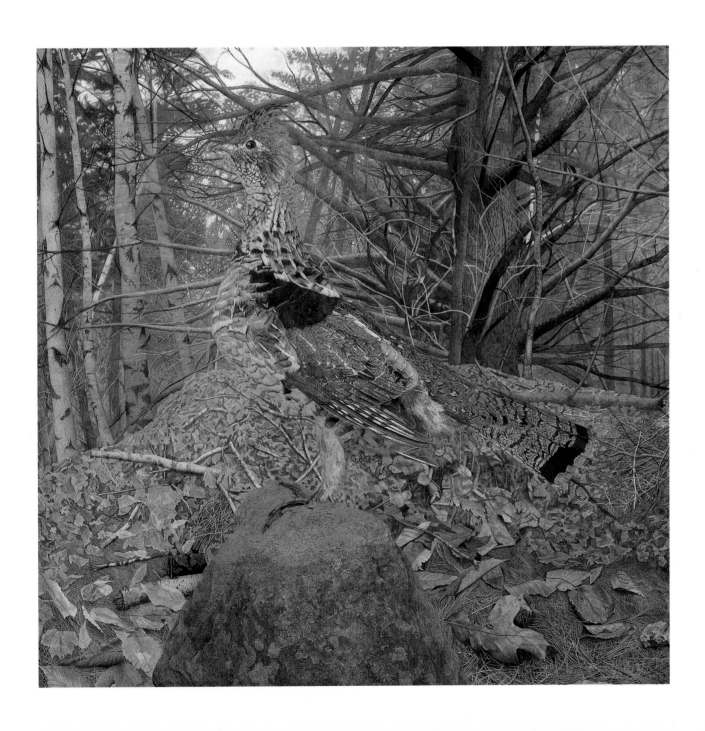

Mayuri. Many musical instruments made in India take animal shapes, and the peacock—an attribute of Sarasvati, goddess of wisdom and music—is a traditional form (*mayuri* is the Sanskrit word for peacock). The hollow body of the nineteenth-century lute (below) acts as a resonator and is made of wood, but the feathers are real. The instrument, originally played only by women, who often sang as they bowed or plucked the strings, is not unlike a viola in tone—quite a contrast to the actual noise made by the peacock, a raucous cry that does no justice to the bird's exceptional beauty. According to Indian legend, however, peacocks were attracted to music and even danced to it.

The Peacocks. Without losing a single detail of natural form, the sculptor Gaston Lachaise (American, 1882–1935) has elegantly stylized three peacocks and arranged them in a geometric design to create the gilded bronze fire screen opposite.

Plumage. The glittering iridescent feathers of the peacock make it one of the wonders of the avian world. In the oil painting below, Priscilla W. Roberts (American, 1916–) has captured the intricate pattern of the peacock's train, which is composed of elongated feathers originating from the bird's lower back. Its real tail lies inconspicuously beneath the train.

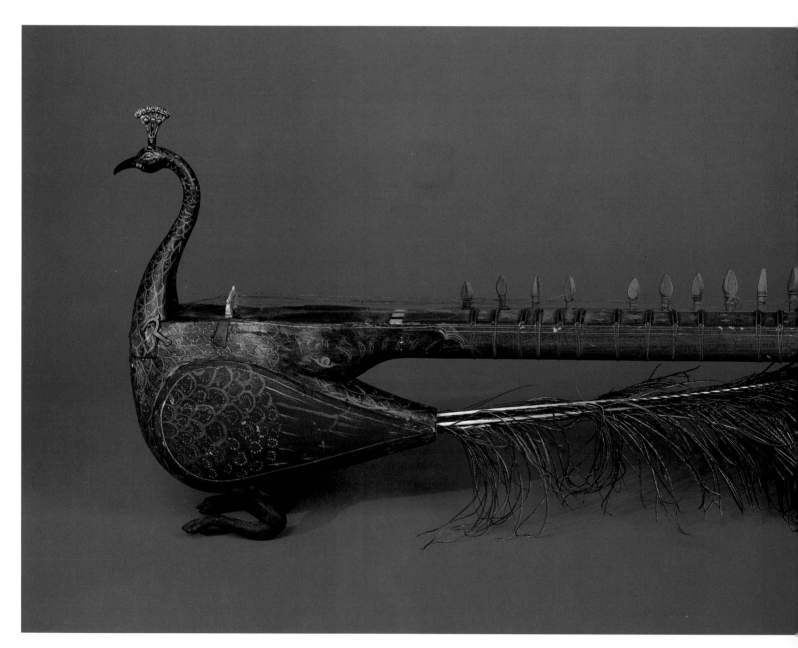

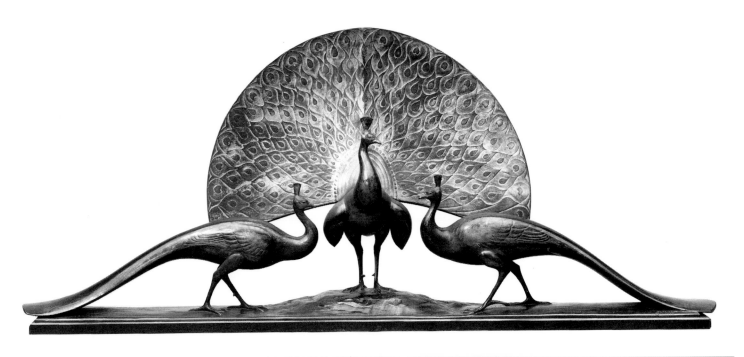

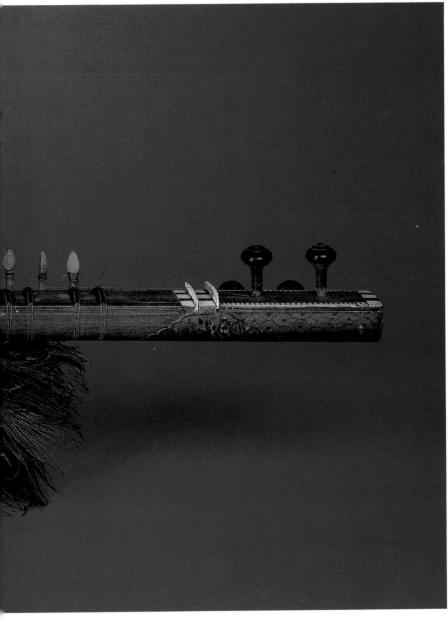

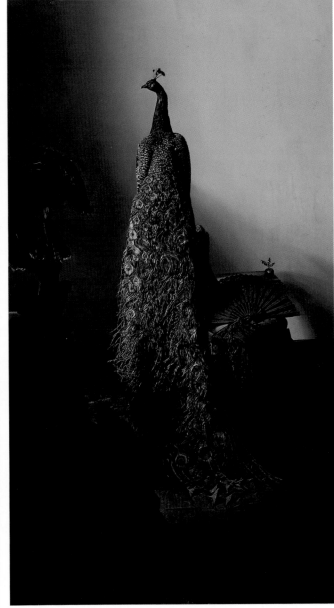

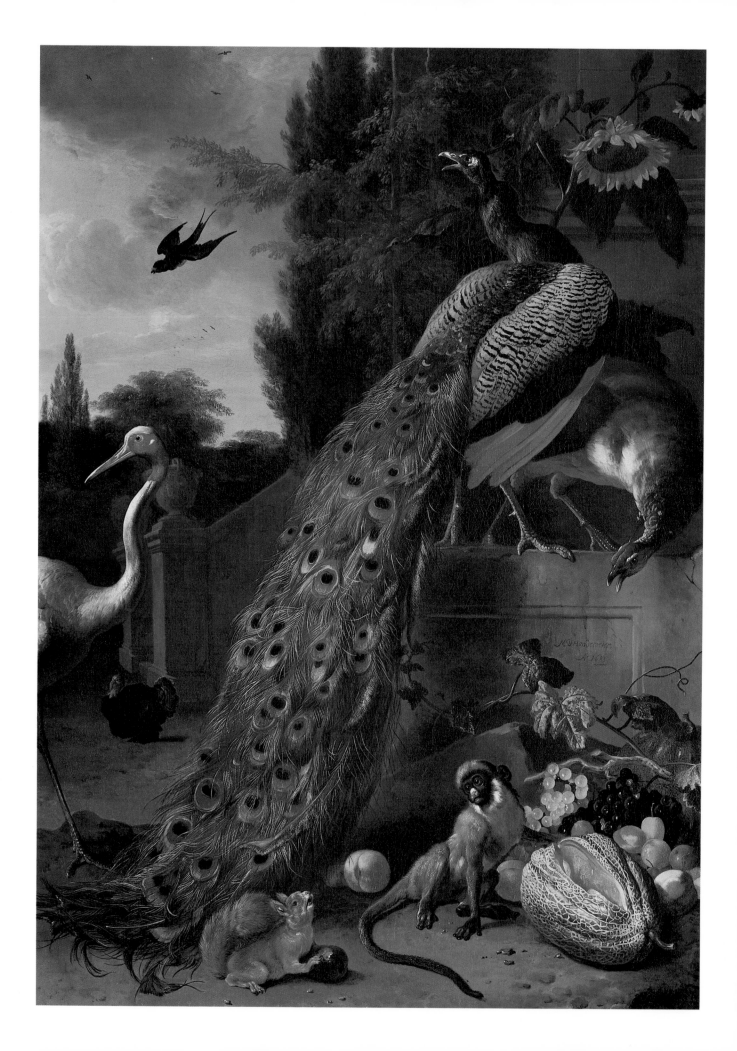

Peacocks. The Dutch artist Melchior d'Hondecoeter (1636–95) demonstrates his special skill in painting ornamental fowl and other wildlife species in this dramatic menagerie scene. Although the peacock overshadows the peahen here, as in nature, both are depicted in meticulous detail, as are the other animals in this incongruous grouping—a flying swallow, a sarus crane, a turkey, a red squirrel, and a vervet monkey (reproduced in detail on page 39). Although the peacock appears in the Bible and in Greek and Roman mythology (as an attribute of the goddess Hera, or Juno), its presence here seems to be primarily decorative.

Peacock Plate. The glazed earthenware plate (below) from Pennsylvania is dated 1793 and carries the initials HR, which probably stand for Henry Roudebuth, a ceramic artist from Montgomery County. Peacocks are native to the hot, humid lowlands of eastern Asia, but they were imported to the Americas long ago, perhaps as early as colonial times, and they have survived well in captivity in the northern climate.

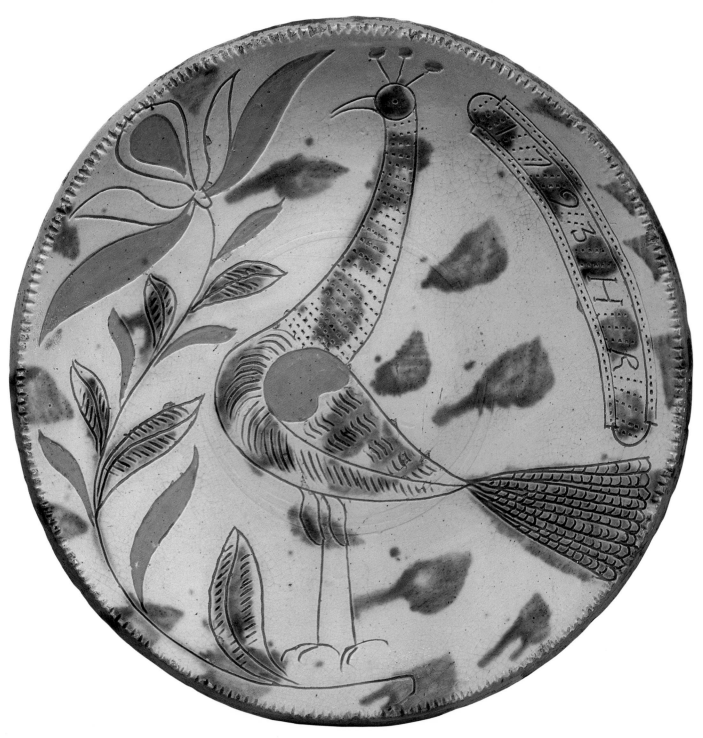

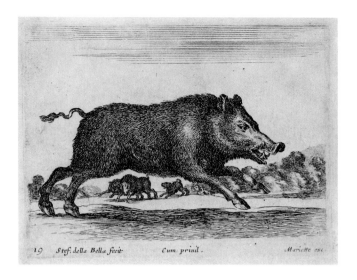

19 Stef. della Bella fecit   Cum privil.   Mariette exc.

List of Illustrations

PAGE 24. *Statuette, Polar Bear*
François Pompon (French, 1855–1933)
White marble with black marble base; 9³⁄₈ in. high
Purchase, Edward C. Moore, Jr. Gift, 1930, 30.123ab

Figure of a Bear and a Tree Stump
America (Central Pennsylvania, 1850–75)
Redware; 6 in. high
Friends of the American Wing Fund, 1980, 1980.357

PAGE 25. *Study of a Bear Walking*
Leonardo da Vinci (Italian, 1452–1519)
Silverpoint on light buff prepared paper; 4¹⁄₁₆ x 5¹⁄₄ in.
Robert Lehman Collection, 1975, 1975.1.369

Bear
J. E. Ridinger (German, 1698–1767)
Engraving; 12³⁄₈ x 8¹⁄₄ in.
The Elisha Whittelsey Collection, The Elisha Whittelsey Fund,
  1958, 58.625.4

Bear Fresco from Church of San Bandelio de Berlanga
Spain (12th century)
Fresco transferred to canvas; 78¹⁄₂ x 44¹⁄₄ in.
The Cloisters Collection, 1957, 57.97.4

PAGE 26. *The Unicorn is Killed or Wounded, and Brought
  to the Castle* (detail)
Franco-Netherlandish (ca. 1500)
Tapestry; 145 x 153 in.
The Cloisters Collection, 1937, 37.80.5

PAGE 27. *Figurine of a Jay with a Squirrel*
Germany (Meissen, ca. 1740)
Hard-paste porcelain, gilt bronze; 18 in. high
The Lesley and Emma Sheafer Collection, Bequest of
  Emma A. Sheafer, 1973, 1974.356.344

PAGE 28. *The Dormouse*
Eric Daglish (British, 1894–1966)
Woodblock print; 4¹⁄₁₆ x 3¹⁄₂ in.
Gift of William M. Lybrand, 1942, 42.33.13

Hudson's Bay Lemming
John Woodhouse Audubon (American, 1812–62)
Oil on canvas; 14¹⁄₄ x 22 in.
Gift of Mrs. Darwin Morse, 1963, 63.200.5

PAGE 29. *Porcupines*
R. W. Chanler (American, 1872–1930)
Oil on panel; 69¹⁄₂ x 48¹⁄₄ in.
Gift of Mrs. John Jay Chapman, 1927, 27.30

PAGE 30. *Kalila wa Dimna, folio 35 verso*
India (mid-16th century)
Ink and colors on paper; average leaf 12¹⁄₂ x 8⁷⁄₈ in.
The Nasli Heeramaneck Collection, Gift of Alice Heeramaneck,
  1981, 1981.373

PAGE 31. *Rabbits on a Log*
Arthur Fitzwilliam Tait (American, 1819–1905)
Oil on canvas; 10 x 12 in.
Gift of Mrs. J. Augustus Barnard, 1979, 1979.490.7

PAGE 32. *Vase in the Form of a Hare*
Greece (Corinthian, first half 6th century B.C.)
Terracotta; 3¹⁄₄ in. long
Gift of Alastair Bradley Martin, 1952, 52.128

Netsuke: Rabbit
Ohara Mitsuhiro (Japanese, 1810–75)
Ivory; 1¹⁄₂ in. high
Edward C. Moore Collection, Bequest of Edward C. Moore, 1891,
  91.1.975

Vase in the Form of a Spotted Hare
Greece (ca. 600–575 B.C.)
Terracotta; 2³⁄₈ x 2¹⁄₂ in.
Funds from various donors, 1923, 23.72.2

Snowbound
Eric Daglish (British, 1894–1966)
Woodblock print; 5¹⁄₂ x 4¹⁄₂ in.
Gift of William M. Lybrand, 1942, 42.33.15

PAGE 33. *The Unicorn at the Fountain* (detail)
Franco-Netherlandish (ca. 1500)
Tapestry; 145 x 149 in.
The Cloisters Collection, 1937, 37.80.2

PAGE 34. *Studies of a Bat and Two Ears*
Jusepe de Ribera (Spanish, 1591–1652)
Red chalk and wash; 6¹⁄₄ x 11 in.
Rogers Fund, 1972, 1972.77

Emperor's Twelve-Symbol Robe (detail)
China (late 18th century)
Silk gauze, embroidered, couched, wrapped gold; 56 in. long
Purchase, Joseph Pulitzer Bequest, 1935, 35.84.8

PAGE 35. *Bat Medallion Robe* (detail)
China (early 18th century)
Embroidered satin; 54 in. long
Anonymous Gift, 1943, 43.119

PAGE 36. *Monkey*
Georges Seurat (French, 1859–91)
Conté crayon; 12¹⁵⁄₁₆ x 9⁵⁄₁₆ in.
Bequest of Miss Adelaide Milton de Groot (1876–1967), 1967,
  67.187.35

PAGE 37. *Face Mask with Monkey*
Mali (Dogon, 19th–20th century)
Wood, paint, rope; 32⁷⁄₈ in. high
The Michael C. Rockefeller Memorial Collection, Bequest of
  Nelson A. Rockefeller, 1964, 1978.412.364

Figure: Baboon
Egypt (Saite-Ptolemaic, Dynasty 26, ca. 664–525 B.C.)
Faïence; 3¹⁄₂ in.
Purchase, Edward S. Harkness Gift, 1926, 26.7.874

PAGE 38. *Two-handled Cup on a Tall Foot in the Form of a Monkey*
Greece (early 5th century B.C.)
Clay; 5³⁄₄ in. high with handles
The Cesnola Collection, Purchased by Subscription, 1874–1876,
  74.51.369

Three Monkeys
Mori Sōsen, in the style of (Japanese, 1747–1821)
Ink on screen; 41 x 15 in.
Charles Stewart Smith Collection, Gift of Mrs. Charles Stewart
  Smith, Charles Stewart Smith, Jr. and Howard Caswell Smith, in
  memory of Charles Stewart Smith, 1914, 14.76.65d

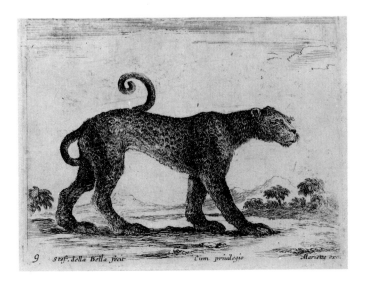

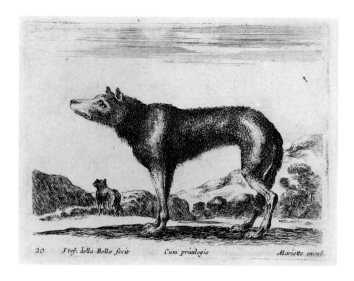

20 Stef. della Bella fecit Cum privilegio Mariette excud.

PAGE 39. *Peacocks* (detail)
Melchior d'Hondecoeter (Dutch, 1636–95)
Oil on canvas; 74⁷/₈ x 53 in.
Gift of Samuel H. Kress, 1927, 27.250.1

PAGES 40–41. *Monkeys*
Suizan Miki (Japanese, 1891–1957)
Ink on screen; 83¹/₂ x 146 in.
Gift of Japan Institute Inc., 1942, 42.39.1b

PAGE 42. *Copy of Wall Painting from Thebes*
Copyist: C. K. Wilkinson
Egypt (Dynasty 18, ca. 1475 B.C.)
Tempera; 29¹/₂ x 41³/₄ in.
Rogers Fund, 1930, 30.4.138

PAGE 43. *The Majestic and Graceful Giraffes, or Cameleopards*
Edward W. Clay for Henry R. Robinson (American, 19th century)
Lithograph; 12 x 15 in.
The Edward W. C. Arnold Collection of New York Prints, Maps,
  and Pictures, Bequest of Edward W. C. Arnold, 1954, 54.90.699

PAGE 44. *Camel Fresco from Church of San Bandelio de Berlanga*
Spain (12th century)
Fresco; 96 x 53¹/₂ in.
The Cloisters Collection, 1961, 61.219

Bactrian Camel
China (Wei dynasty, 6th century)
Unglazed pottery; 9³/₄ in. high
Rogers Fund, 1928, 28.121

PAGE 45. *Bowl*
Iraq (Abbased period, 10th century)
Earthenware, glazed and luster painted; 9 in. diameter
Purchase, Joseph Pulitzer Bequest, 1964, 64.259

PAGE 46. *Deer in the Snow, Moonlight,* or *The Stag in Winter*
William Morris Hunt (American, 1824–79)
Lithograph; 9³/₄ x 6⁷/₁₆ in.
Gift of Otto Hufeland, 1908, 08.2

PAGE 47. *Two Stags Running*
Sir Edwin Henry Landseer (British, 1802–73)
Brush and brown wash on brownish paper; 4³/₈ x 5¹³/₁₆ in.
Bequest of Mary Cushing Fosburgh, 1978, 1979.135.7

Dish with Large Deer
Spain (15th century)
Tin enameled earthenware decorated in blue and copper luster;
  18 in. diameter
The Cloisters Collection, 1956, 56.171.71

PAGE 48. *Head of a Horned Animal*
Iran (Achaemenid period, 6th–4th century B.C.)
Bronze; 13³/₈ in. high
Fletcher Fund, 1956, 56.45

PAGE 49. *Figure of Dignity: Irish Mountain Goat*
John B. Flannagan (American, 1895–1942)
Granite and aluminum horns; 53³/₄ in. high with base
Gift of Alexander Shilling Fund, 1941, 41.47

Antelope Headdresses
Mali (Bamana, 19th–20th century)
Wood, metal bands; 35³/₄ and 28 in. high
The Michael C. Rockefeller Memorial Collection, Bequest of
  Nelson A. Rockefeller, 1964, 1978.412.435,6

PAGE 50. *A Gazelle*
Unknown Lombard artist (Italian, beginning of 15th century)
Silverpoint, pen and ink with additional colors in brush on vellum;
  4 x 5 in.
Robert Lehman Collection, 1975, 1975.1.402

PAGE 51. *Figure: Gazelle*
Egypt (Thebes, late Dynasty 18, ca. 1379–1362 B.C.)
Ivory, wood, and Egyptian blue pigment; 4¹/₂ in. high
Purchase, Edward S. Harkness Gift, 1926, 26.7.1292

Cup with Four Gazelles
Northwest Iran (ca. 1000 B.C.)
Gold; 2⁹/₁₆ in. high, 3³/₈ in. diameter
Rogers Fund, 1962, 62.84

Nilgai, Leaf from an Album of Shah Jahan
India (Mughal, 1605–27)
Ink, colors, and gold on paper; 15⁵/₁₆ x 10¹/₁₆ in.
Purchase, Rogers Fund and The Kevorkian Foundation Gift, 1955,
  55.121.13

PAGE 52. *Netsuke: Boar*
Tomotada (Japanese, Edo period, 1615–1867)
Ivory; 2¹/₄ in. long
Bequest of Stephen Whitney Phoenix, 1881, 81.8.91

Wild Pig
J. E. Ridinger (German, 1698–1767)
Engraving; 14³/₄ x 11³/₄ in.
The Elisha Whittelsey Collection, The Elisha Whittelsey Fund,
  1958, 58.625.1

Vessel in the Form of a Boar
Southwest Iran (ca. 2900 B.C.)
Ceramic; 5³/₄ in. high
Purchase, Rogers Fund and Anonymous Gift, 1979, 1979.71

PAGE 53. *Volute Krater: Two Boars*
Attributed to Sophilos (Greek, Attic, early 6th century B.C.)
Black-figured vase; 19³/₈ in. high (as restored with modern foot)
Purchase, Mr. and Mrs. Martin Fried Gift, 1977, 1977.11.2

PAGE 54. *Bark Painting: Two Kangaroos*
Australia (Northern Territory, Arnhem Land, Oenpelli area,
  20th century)
Bark, paint; 40¹/₂ in. high
The Michael C. Rockefeller Memorial Collection, Bequest of
  Nelson A. Rockefeller, 1979, 1979.206.1514

PAGE 55. *Figure of a Hippopotamus from Tomb of Senbi at Meir*
Egypt (Dynasty 12, ca. 1991–1786 B.C.)
Blue faïence; 4³/₈ in. high
Gift of Edward S. Harkness, 1917, 17.9.1

Water Buffalo
China (Sung dynasty or later, 12th century)
Dark green jade; 5⁷/₈ in. high
Gift of Mrs. Edward S. Harkness, 1936, 36.121

PAGE 56. *Rhinoceros Figurines*
Ralph Wood (English, 18th century)
Glazed pottery; 6¹/₂ and 6¹/₄ in. high
Gift of Mrs. Russell S. Carter, 1944, 44.39.58,9

The Rhinoceros
Albrecht Dürer (German, 1471–1528)
Woodblock print; 8³/₈ x 11⁵/₈ in.
Gift of Junius S. Morgan, 1919, 19.73.159

PAGE 57. *Rhinoceros Platter*
England (Chelsea, 1752–56)
Porcelain; 9³/₄ x 12³/₄ in.
Gift of Irwin Untermyer, 1964, 64.101.482

PAGE 58. *Histoire Naturelle des Deux Elephans*, 1803 (plate)
J. P. L. L. Houel (French, 1735–1813)
Engraving; 14 x 10³/₄ in.
The Elisha Whittelsey Collection, The Elisha Whittelsey Fund,
  1953, 53.554.5

PAGE 59. *Elephant*
Stefano della Bella (Italian, 1610–64)
Etching; 3¹/₂ x 9⁷/₁₆ in.
Purchase, Joseph Pulitzer Bequest, 1917, 17.50.17-259

Histoire Naturelle des Deux Elephans, 1803 (plate)
J. P. L. L. Houel (French, 1735–1813)
Engraving; 14 x 10³/₄ in.
The Elisha Whittelsey Collection, The Elisha Whittelsey Fund,
  1953, 53.554.5

PAGE 60. *Senegalese Elephant*
Antoine-Louis Barye (French, 1796–1875)
Bronze; 5¹/₂ in. high
Bequest of Jacob Ruppert, 1939, 39.65.58a

PAGE 61. *Buddhist Priest's Robe* (detail)
China (K'ang-hsi period, ca. 1661–1772)
Woven silk, metal thread, peacock feathers, filaments (K'o sso);
  42 x 102¹/₂ in.
Gift of Mrs. Maurice Casalis, 1945, 45.123.4

PAGE 62. *Writing Case with Cover*
Japan (19th century)
Black, gold lacquer, mother of pearl; 9³/₄ x 8 in.
Bequest of Benjamin Altman, 1913, 14.40.838ab

PAGE 63. *Insect Study*
Joris Hoefnagel (Flemish, 1542–1600) or Jacob Hoefnagel
  (1575–1630)
Pen, brown ink, colored washes, and gold paint on vellum;
  4³/₄ x 6³/₁₆ in.
Gift of Mrs. Darwin Morse, 1963, 63.200.4

PAGE 64. *Spider from Album of Flower and Bird Paintings*
Katei (Japanese, 1830–1901)
Ink and colors on silk; 10 x 12 in.
Gift of Dr. and Mrs. Harold B. Bilsky, 1975, 1975.282.1h

PAGE 65. *Beetle Watch*
Switzerland (mid-19th century)
Gold, partly enameled, and jewels; 2¹/₈ in. long
Bequest of Laura Frances Hearn, 1917, 17.101.55

Crayfish Pendant
Panama (Chiriqui, 11th–16th century)
Gold; 2¹/₈ in. long
The Michael C. Rockefeller Memorial Collection, Bequest of
  Nelson A. Rockefeller, 1979, 1979.206.1053

PAGE 66. *Stirrup Jar: Octopus and Other Fish*
Greece (Mycenaean, 1200–1125 B.C.)
Terracotta; 10¹/₄ in. high
Purchase, Louisa Eldridge McBurney Gift, 1953, 53.11.6

PAGE 67. *Ceremonial Coverlet*
Japan (19th century)
Cotton; 63¹/₂ x 58¹/₂ in.
Seymour Fund, 1966, 66.239.3

PAGES 68-69. *Underwater Marine Life*
Christian Schuessele (American, 1824/6–79) and
  James M. Sommerville
Watercolor; 18⁷/₈ x 27¹/₂ in.
Gift of Mr. and Mrs. Erving Wolf, 1977, 1977.181

PAGE 70. *Fish Plate*
Greece (Campanian, late 4th century B.C.)
Terracotta; 10⁷/₈ in. diameter
Rogers Fund, 1906, 06.1021.243

PAGE 71. *Gruel Bowl in the Form of a Fish*
France (Mennecy, 1745)
Soft-paste porcelain; 8¹/₄ in. long
Gift of R. Thornton Wilson, in memory of
  Florence Ellsworth Wilson, 1954, 54.147.8

The Pleasure of the Fishes (detail)
Chon Tung Ch'ing (Chinese, late Sung to early Yüan dynasty,
  late 13th century)
Handscroll, colors on paper; 12¹/₈ x 233³/₄ in.
Fletcher Fund, 1947, 47.18.10

PAGE 72. *Frog on a Lotus Leaf*
Hsiang Sheng-mo (Chinese, 1597–1658)
Ink and colors on paper; 11¹/₈ x 8¹³/₁₆ in.
Edward Elliott Family Collection, Purchase, The Dillon Fund Gift,
  1981, 1981.285.36

PAGE 73. *Frog Pendant*
Panama (Chiriqui, 11th–16th century)
Gold; 3⁵/₈ in. high
Gift of H. L. Bache Foundation, 1969, 69.7.4

Frog Automaton
Switzerland (19th century)
Gold and enamel; 2⁷/₁₆ in. long
Gift of Murtogh D. Guinness, 1976, 1976.285.2

PAGE 74. *Mi Gyaun (Crocodile Zither)*
Burma (19th century)
Wood; 54 in. long
The Crosby Brown Collection of Musical Instruments,
  1889, 89.4.1473

Crocodiles
John Singer Sargent (American, 1856–1925)
Watercolor; 15³/₄ x 20⁷/₈ in.
Gift of Mrs. Francis Ormond, 1950, 50.130.63

PAGE 75. *Door*
Mali (Bamana or Bozo, 19th–20th century)
Wood, metal; 84¹/₂ in. high
The Michael C. Rockefeller Memorial Collection, Bequest of
  Nelson A. Rockefeller, 1979, 1979.206.155

Butter Box in the Form of a Turtle
Germany (Meissen, ca. 1725)
Hard-paste porcelain; 7¹/₂ in. long
The Jack and Belle Linsky Collection, 1982, 1982.60.324

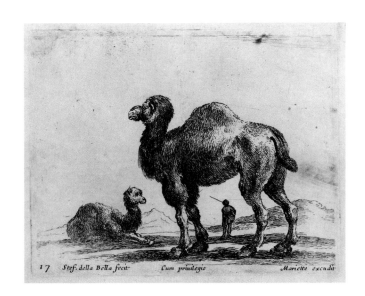

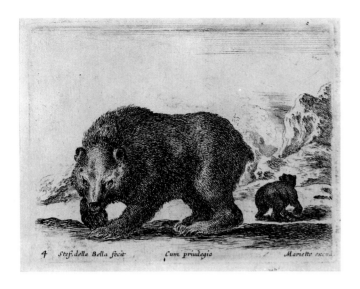

PAGE 76. *Rat Snake, Plate X from Ehon mushi erabi*
Kitagawa Utamaro (Japanese, 1753–1806)
Woodblock print, colors on paper; 10¹/₂ x 7¹/₄ in.
The Howard Mansfield Collection, Gift of Howard Mansfield,
  1936, JP 1052

PAGE 77. *Lair of the Sea Serpent*
Elihu Vedder (American, 1836–1923)
Oil on canvas; 12 x 30 in.
Gift of Mrs. Harold G. Henderson, 1976, 1976.106.1

Cobra Snake
Jean Dunand (French, 1877–1942)
Bronze, partly gilt; 12 in. high
Rogers Fund, 1970, 1970.198.8

Votive Snake
Colombia (Muisca, 10th–16th century)
Gold; 6³/₈ in. long
Gift and Bequest of Alice K. Bache, 1974 and 1977, 1974.271.27

Votive Snake
Colombia (Muisca, 10th–16th century)
Gold; 4⁷/₈ in. long
The Michael C. Rockefeller Memorial Collection, Bequest of
  Nelson A. Rockefeller, 1979, 1979.206.740

PAGES 78–79. *Aquatic Birds at a Pool, Miniature from an Album*
India (Mughal period, late 17th or early 18th century)
Ink and colors on paper; 13¹/₈ x 8¹/₄ in.
Theodore M. Davis Collection, Bequest of Theodore M. Davis,
  1915, 30.95.174 min. #3

PAGE 80. *The Concourse of the Birds*
Habib Allah (Iranian, Safavid period, ca. 1600)
Ink, colors, silver, and gold on paper; 10 x 4¹/₂ in.
Fletcher Fund, 1963, 63.210.11

PAGE 81. *Japanese Crane from Album of Flower and Bird Paintings*
Katei (Japanese, 1830–1901)
Ink and colors on silk; 10 x 12 in.
Gift of Dr. and Mrs. Harold B. Bilsky, 1975, 1975.282.1b

PAGE 82. *Peach Tree, Peonies, and Cranes*
Shen Ch'uan (Chinese, 18th century)
Hanging scroll, colors on silk; 78¹/₄ x 39³/₄ in.
The Harry G. C. Packard Collection of Asian Art, Gift of
  Harry G. C. Packard and Purchase, Fletcher, Rogers,
  Harris Brisbane Dick and Louis V. Bell Funds, Joseph Pulitzer
  Bequest and The Annenberg Fund, Inc. Gift, 1975, 1975.268.81

PAGE 83. *Tureens in the Form of a Pair of Woodcocks*
Germany (18th century)
Faïence; 10 in. high
The Lesley and Emma Sheafer Collection, Bequest of
  Emma A. Scheafer, 1973, 1974.356.241,2

Herons
Maruyama Okyo, in the style of (Japanese, Edo period, 1733–95)
Hanging scroll, ink on paper; 47¹/₂ x 25⁷/₈ in.
The Harry G. C. Packard Collection of Asian Art, Gift of
  Harry G. C. Packard and Purchase, Fletcher, Rogers,
  Harris Brisbane Dick and Louis V. Bell Funds, Joseph Pulitzer
  Bequest and The Annenberg Fund, Inc. Gift, 1975, 1975.268.71

PAGES 84–85. *Angry Swan*
Jean-Baptiste Oudry (French, 1686–1755)
Black and white chalk on blue paper; 9³/₄ x 15 in.
The Mr. and Mrs. Henry Ittleson, Jr. Purchase Fund, 1970,
  1970.133

PAGE 86. *Three Swans*
John Singer Sargent (American, 1856–1925)
Pencil on paper; 6¹/₈ x 9¹/₂ in.
Gift of Mrs. Francis Ormond, 1950, 50.130.142n

PAGE 87. *Wild Ducks in the Snow*
Andō Hiroshige (Japanese, 1797–1858)
Woodblock print; 14⁷/₈ x 6³/₄ in.
Bequest of Mrs. H. O. Havemeyer, 1929, H. O. Havemeyer
  Collection, JP 1894

Vase in the Form of a Swan
Greece (Corinthian, 6th century B.C.)
Terracotta; 4¹/₁₆ in. high
Gift of Schimmel Foundation, Inc., 1980, 1980.427.4

Vase in the Form of a Duck
Greece (mid-6th century B.C.)
Terracotta; 2³/₈ in. high
Rogers Fund, 1913, 13.225.11

PAGE 89. *Woman with a Parrot*
Edouard Manet (French, 1832–83)
Oil on canvas; 72⁷/₈ x 50⁵/₈ in.
Gift of Erwin Davis, 1889, 89.21.3

Finial in the Form of a Parrot
India (late 18th century)
Brass; 5³/₄ in. high
Gift of Robert W. and Lockwood de Forest, 1919, 19.135.3

Woman with a Parrot (detail)
Edouard Manet (French, 1832–83)
Oil on canvas; 72⁷/₈ x 50⁵/₈ in.
Gift of Erwin Davis, 1889, 89.21.3

PAGE 90. *Ivory-billed Woodpeckers*
Attributed to J. B. Kidd (Scottish, 1808–89)
Oil on canvas; 39¹/₄ x 26¹/₂ in.
Rogers Fund, 1941, 41.18

PAGE 91. *Hornbill, Leaf from an Album of Shah Jahan*
India (Mughal period, 1605–27)
Ink, colors, and gold on paper; 15¹/₄ x 10¹/₂ in.
Purchase, Rogers Fund and The Kevorkian Foundation Gift, 1955,
  55.121.14

The Ostrich Hunt
Stefano della Bella (Italian, 1610–64)
Etching; 6³/₈ x 8⁵/₈ in.
The Elisha Whittelsey Collection, The Elisha Whittelsey Fund,
  1957, 57.585.6

PAGE 92. *Vultures on a Tree*
Antoine-Louis Barye (French, 1796–1875)
Watercolor and gouache; 10¹¹/₁₆ x 15¹/₈ in.
Bequest of Mrs. H. O. Havemeyer, 1929, H. O. Havemeyer
  Collection, 29.100.596

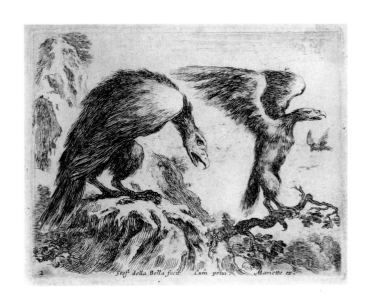

111

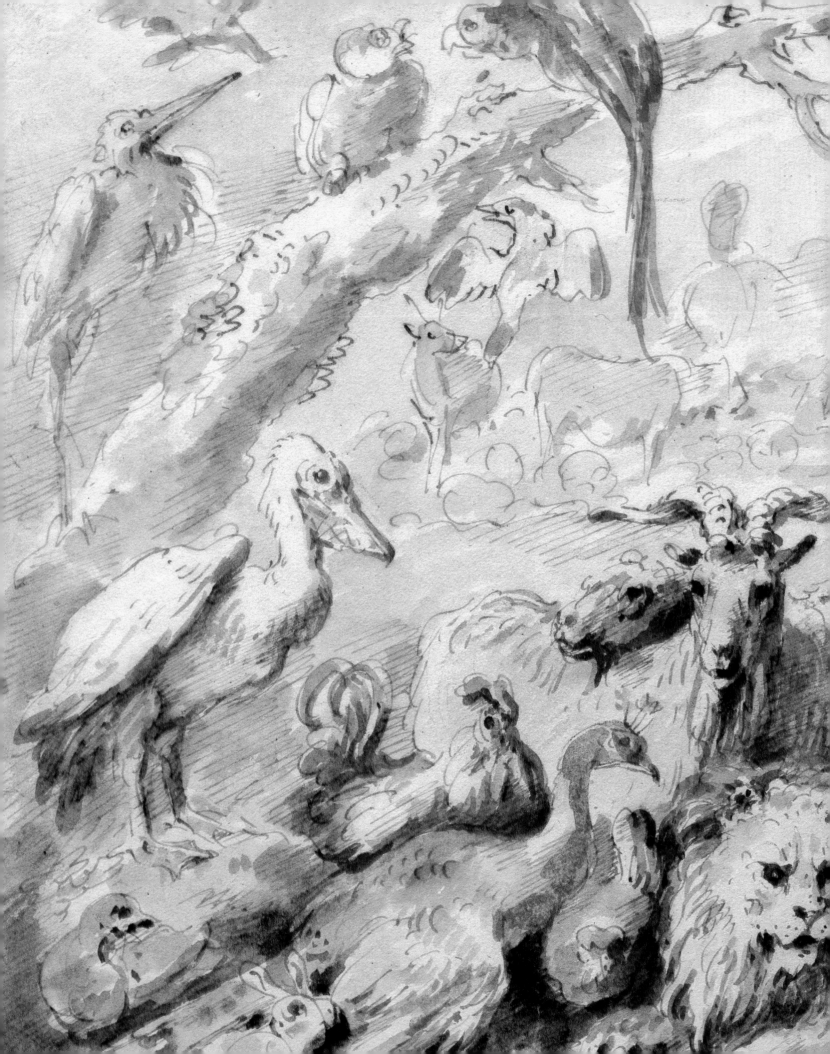